I0462175

Real World
Colouring Book
For Advanced Users & Adults

50 Images

**Created From Real Life Photos
For You To Colour As You Please.**

ISBN 978-0-359-86530-7
90000
9 780359 865307

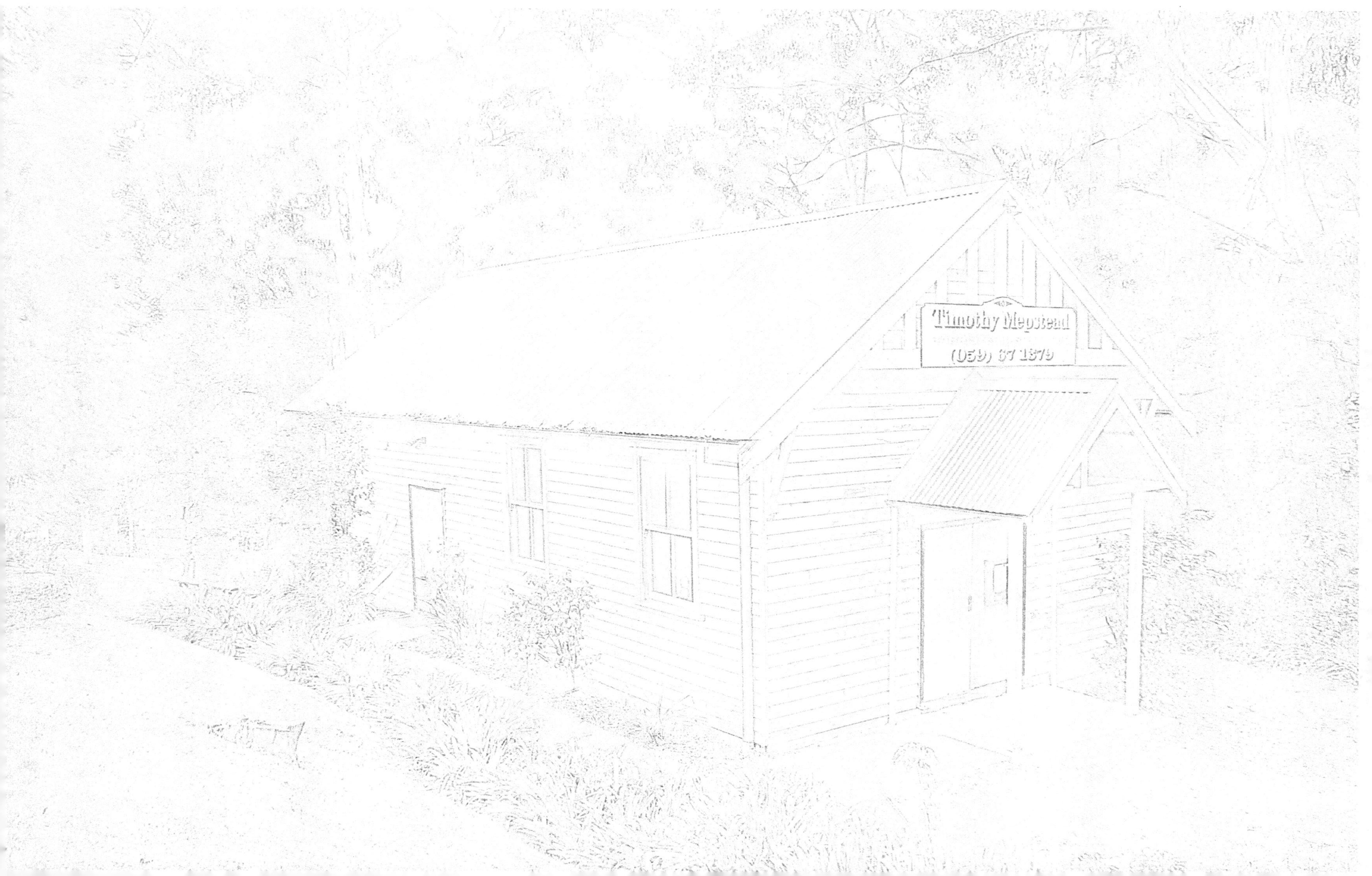
Timothy Megstead
(059) 67 1379

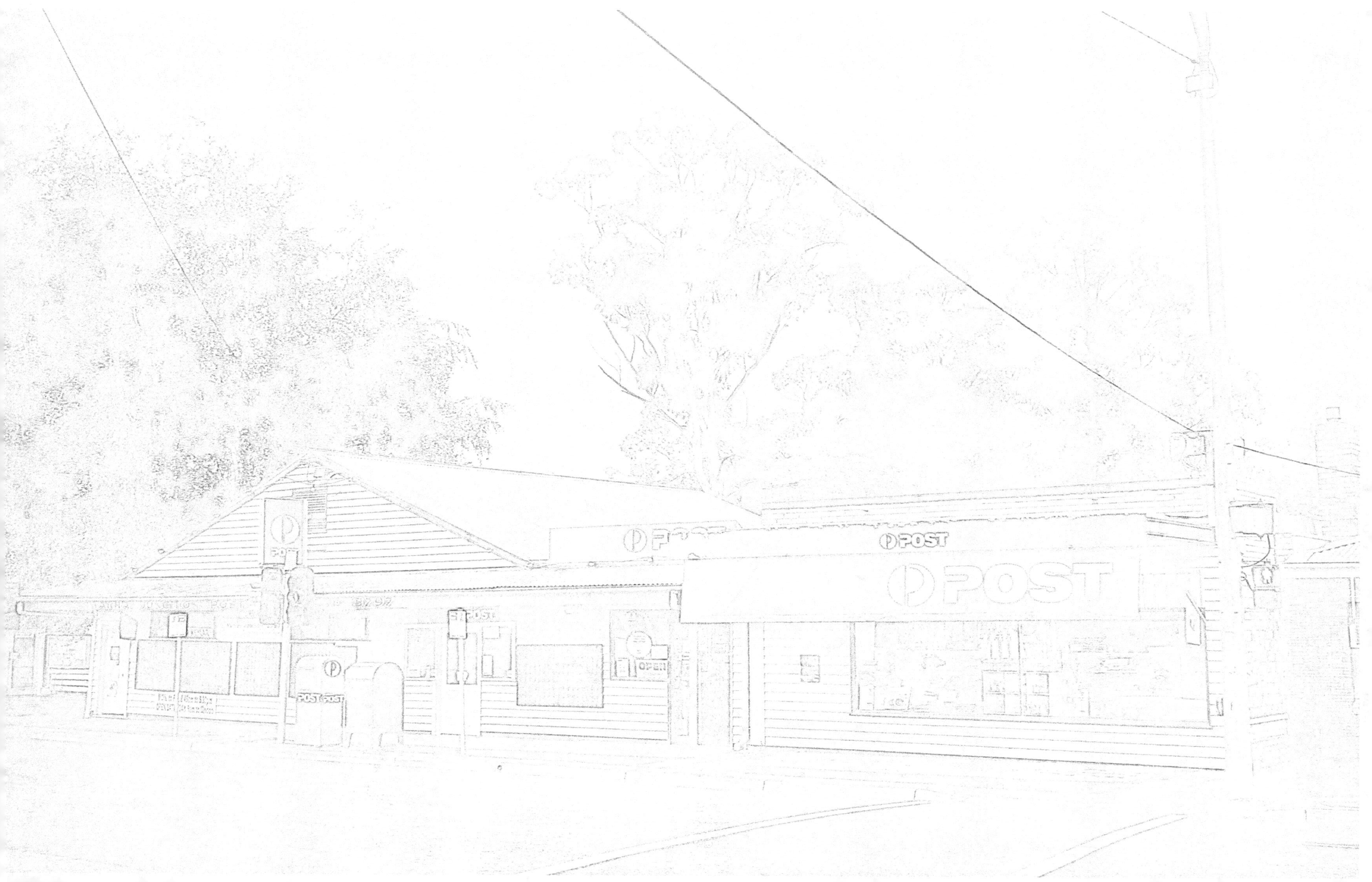
POST
POST
OPEN
POST POST

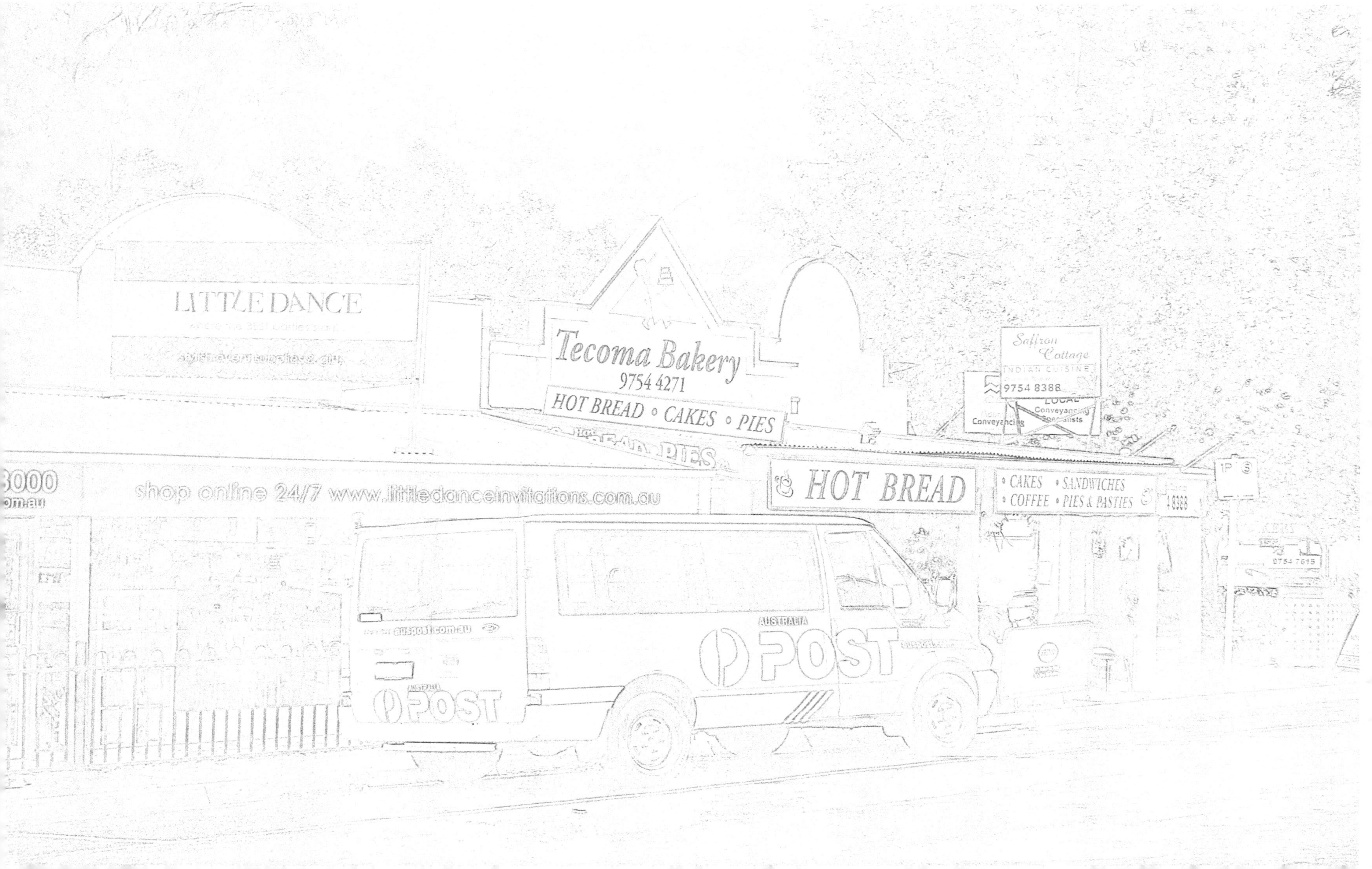
LITTLE DANCE
Tecoma Bakery
9754 4271
HOT BREAD • CAKES • PIES
Saffron Cottage
INDIAN CUISINE
9754 8388
LOCAL Conveyancing Specialists
Conveyancing
shop online 24/7 www.littledanceinvitations.com.au
HOT BREAD
• CAKES • SANDWICHES
• COFFEE • PIES & PASTIES
1P
AUSTRALIA POST
auspost.com.au
9754 7615

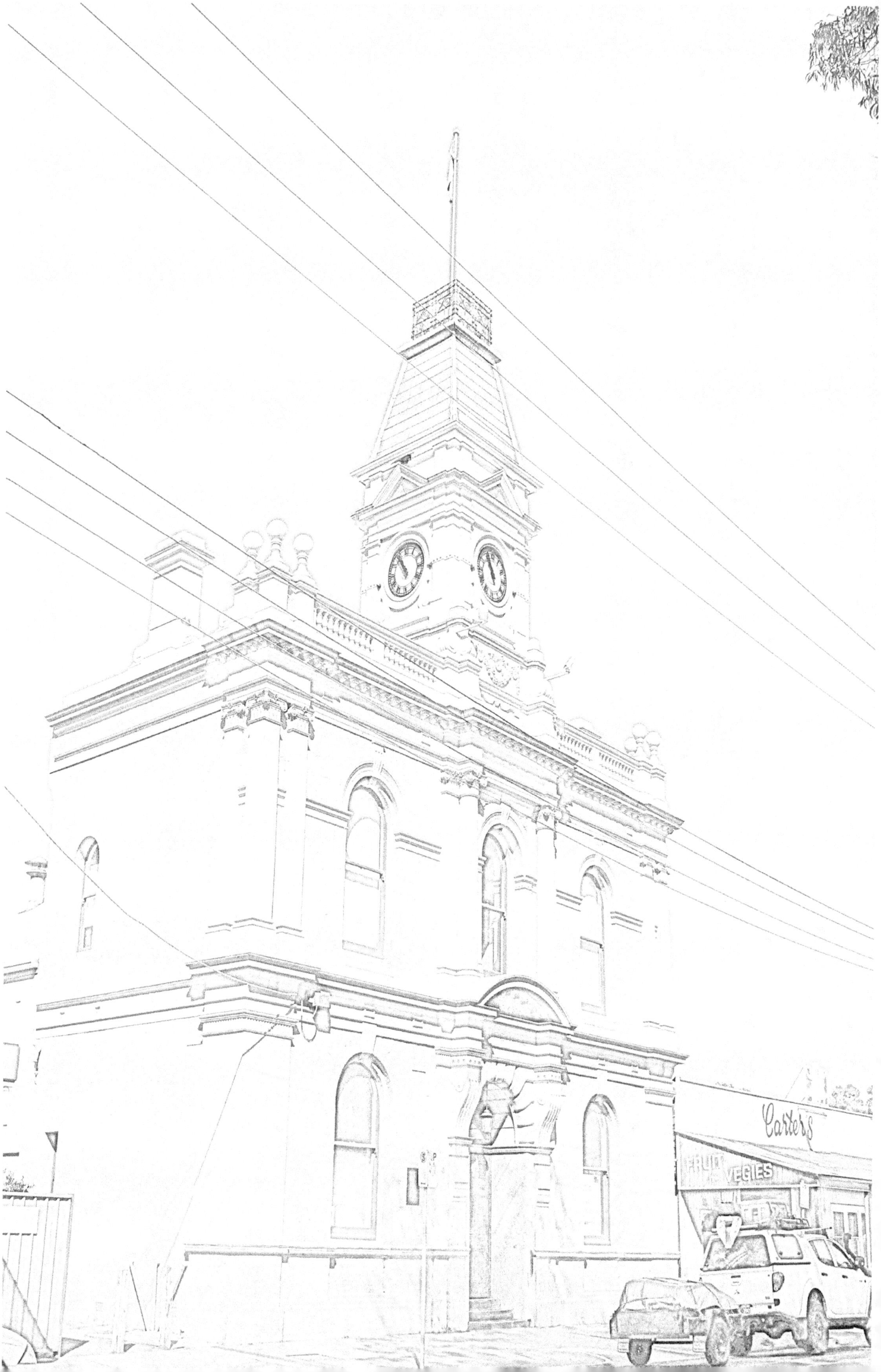
Carter's
FRUIT
VEGIES

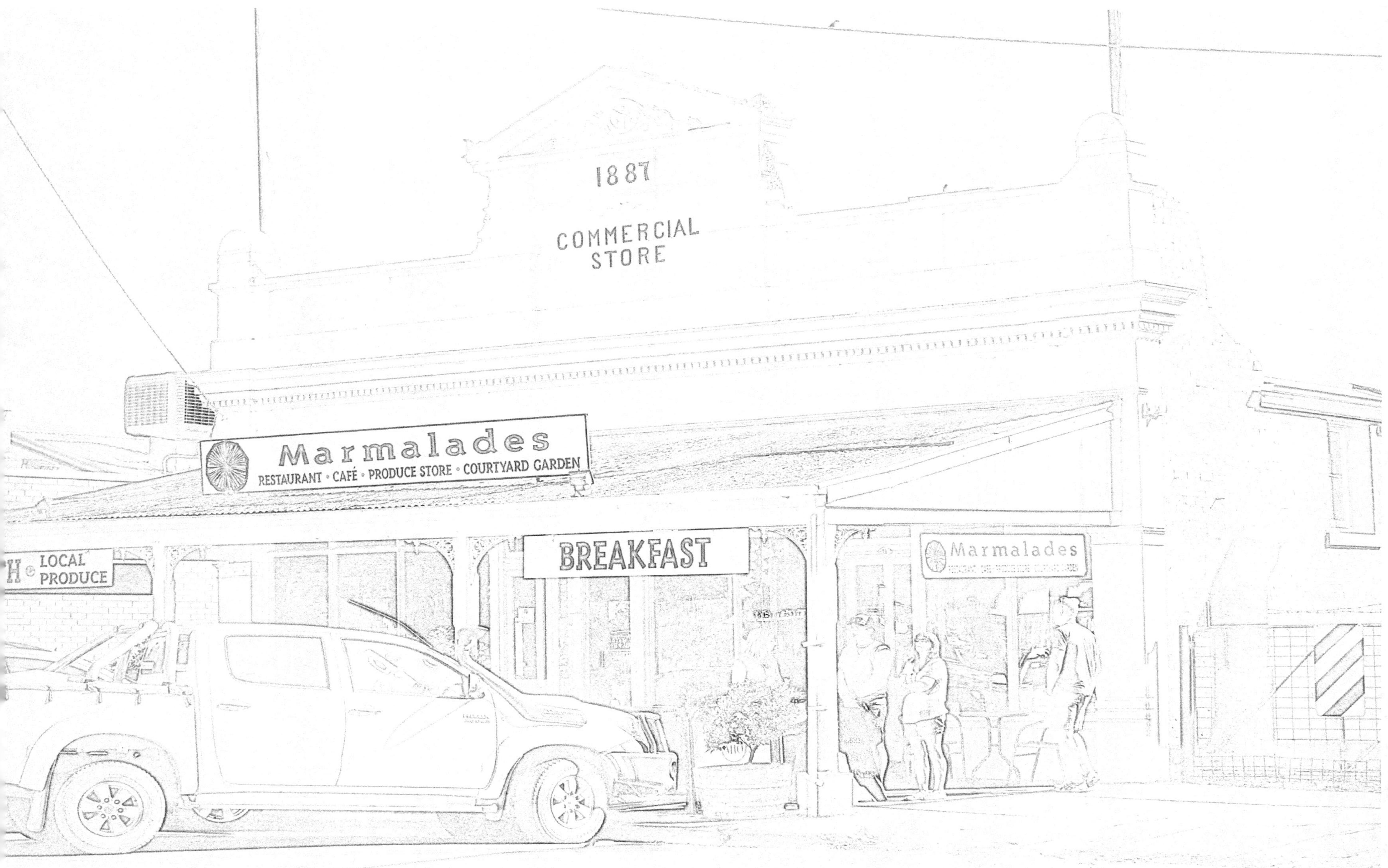
1887
COMMERCIAL
STORE
Marmalades
RESTAURANT • CAFÉ • PRODUCE STORE • COURTYARD GARDEN
BREAKFAST
LOCAL
PRODUCE
Marmalades

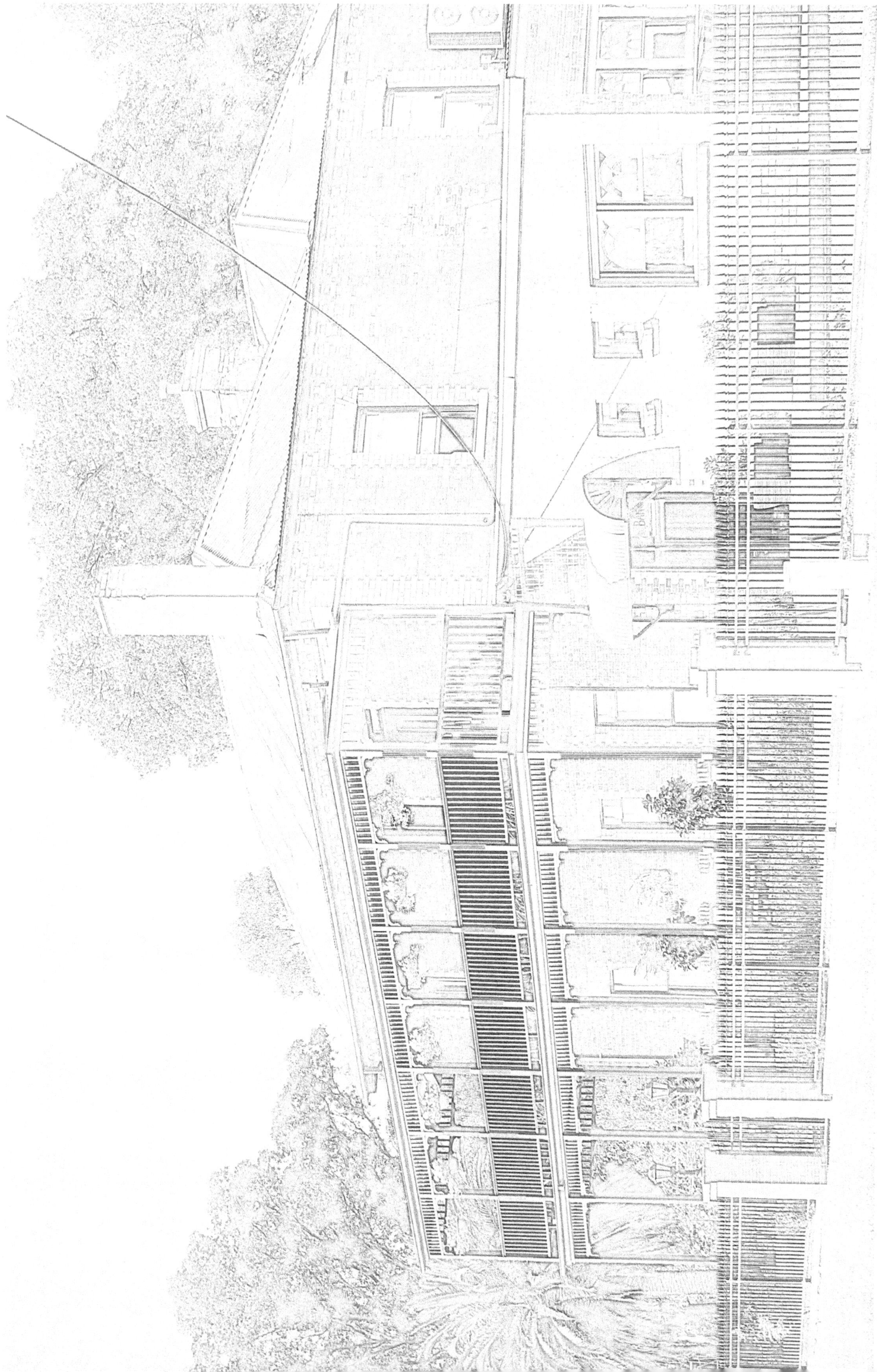

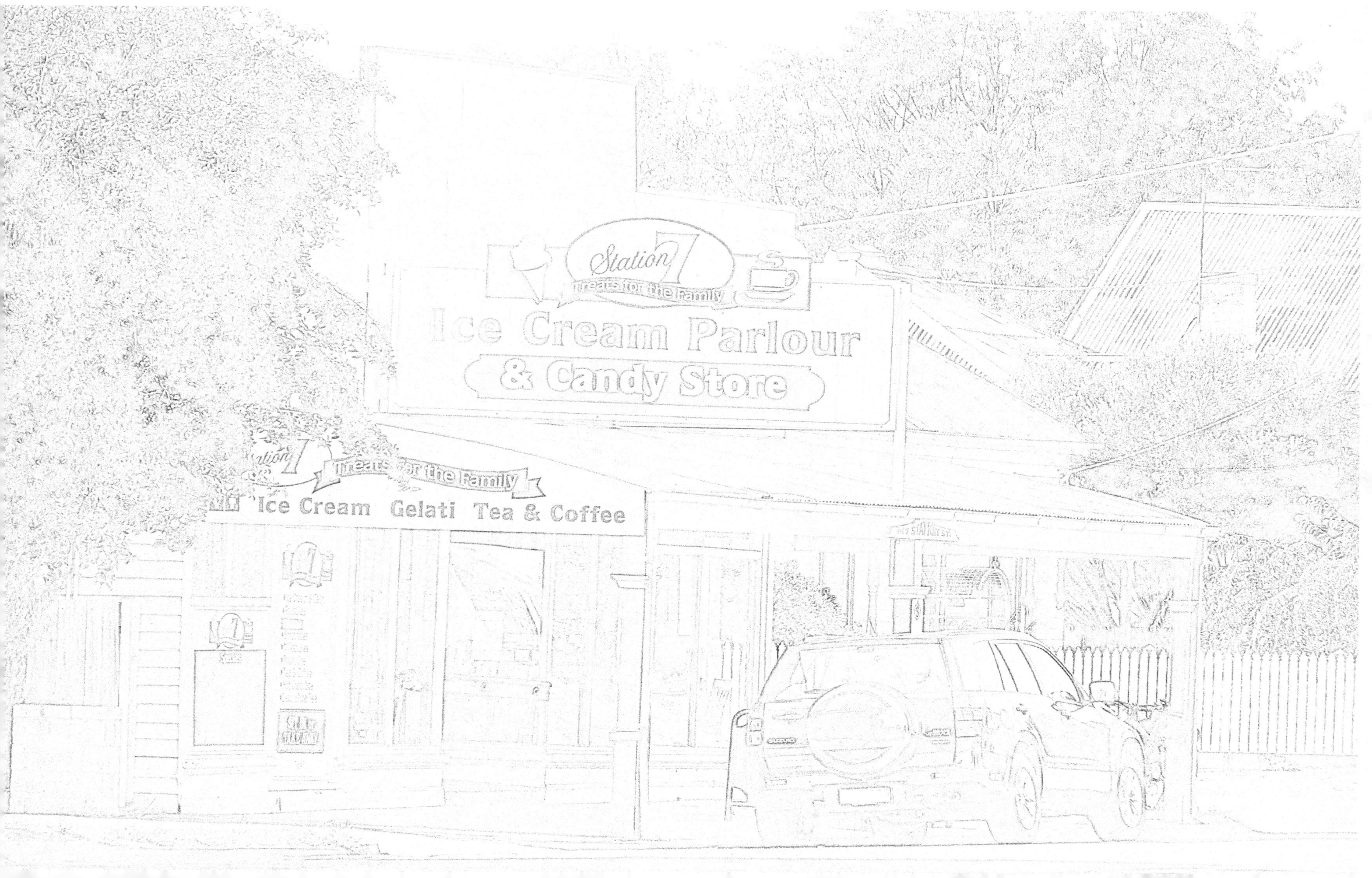
Station 7
Treats for the Family
Ice Cream Parlour
& Candy Store
Station 7
Treats for the Family
Ice Cream Gelati Tea & Coffee

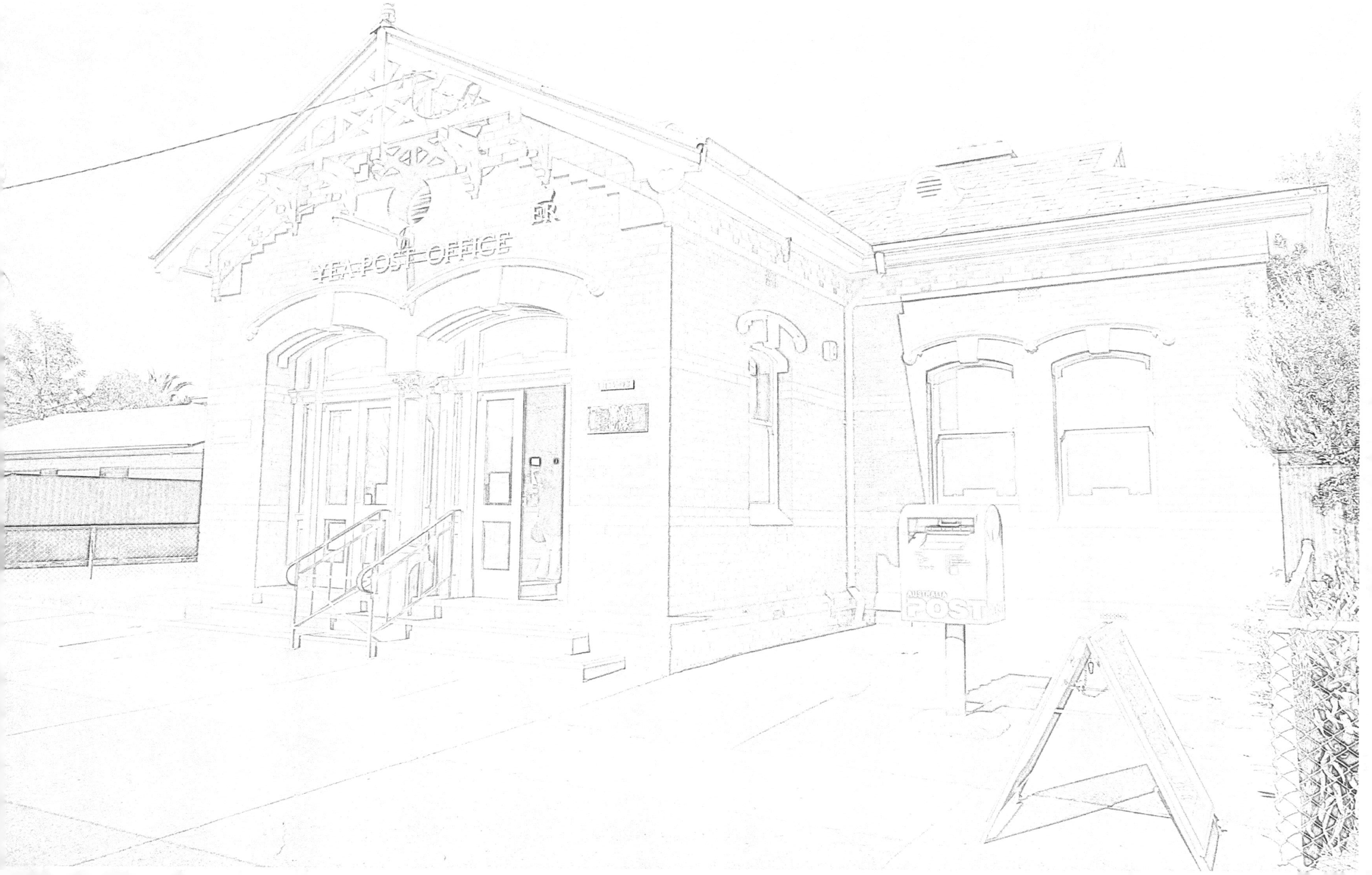
YEA POST OFFICE
ER
AUSTRALIA
POST

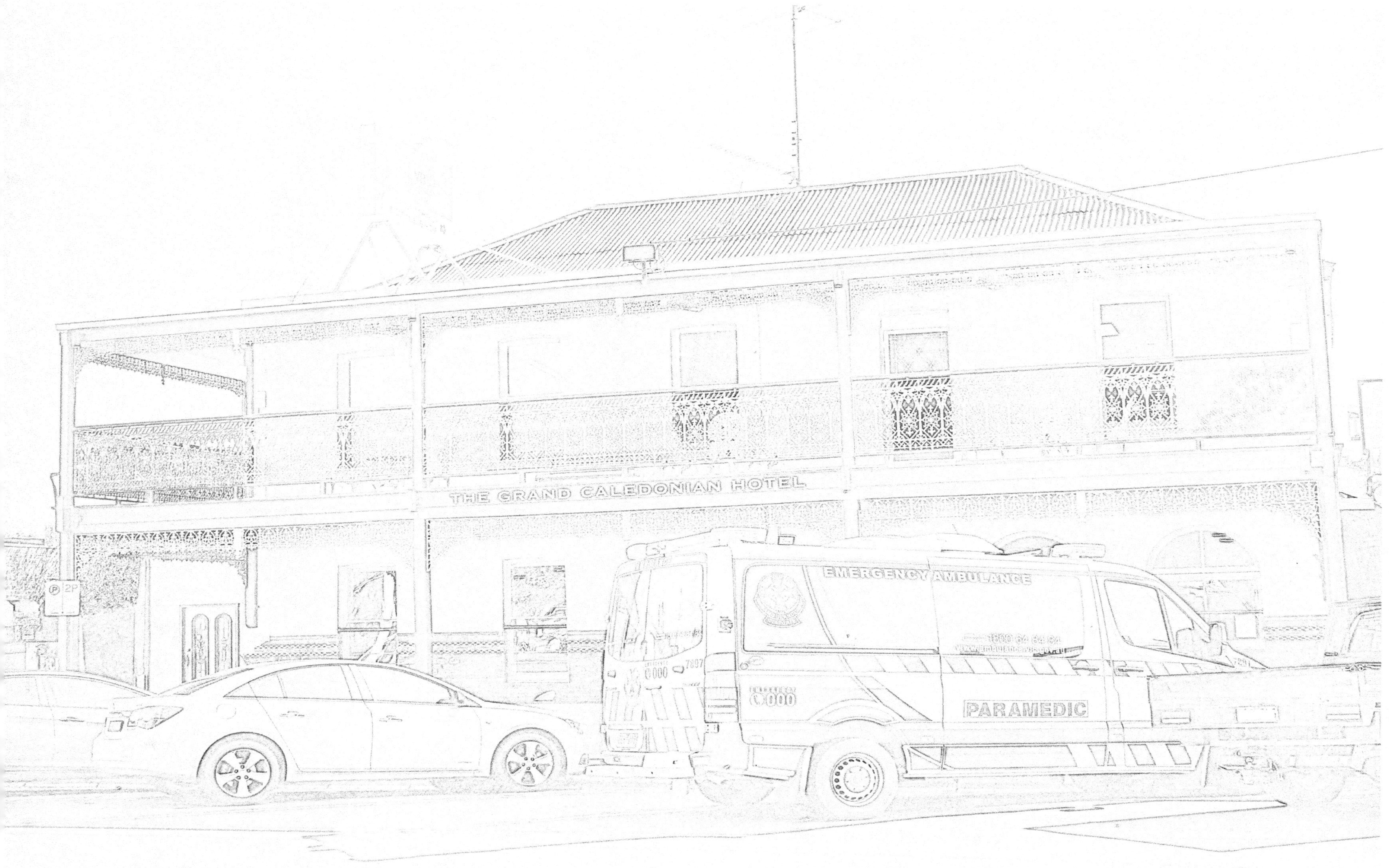
THE GRAND CALEDONIAN HOTEL
EMERGENCY AMBULANCE
PARAMEDIC
2P

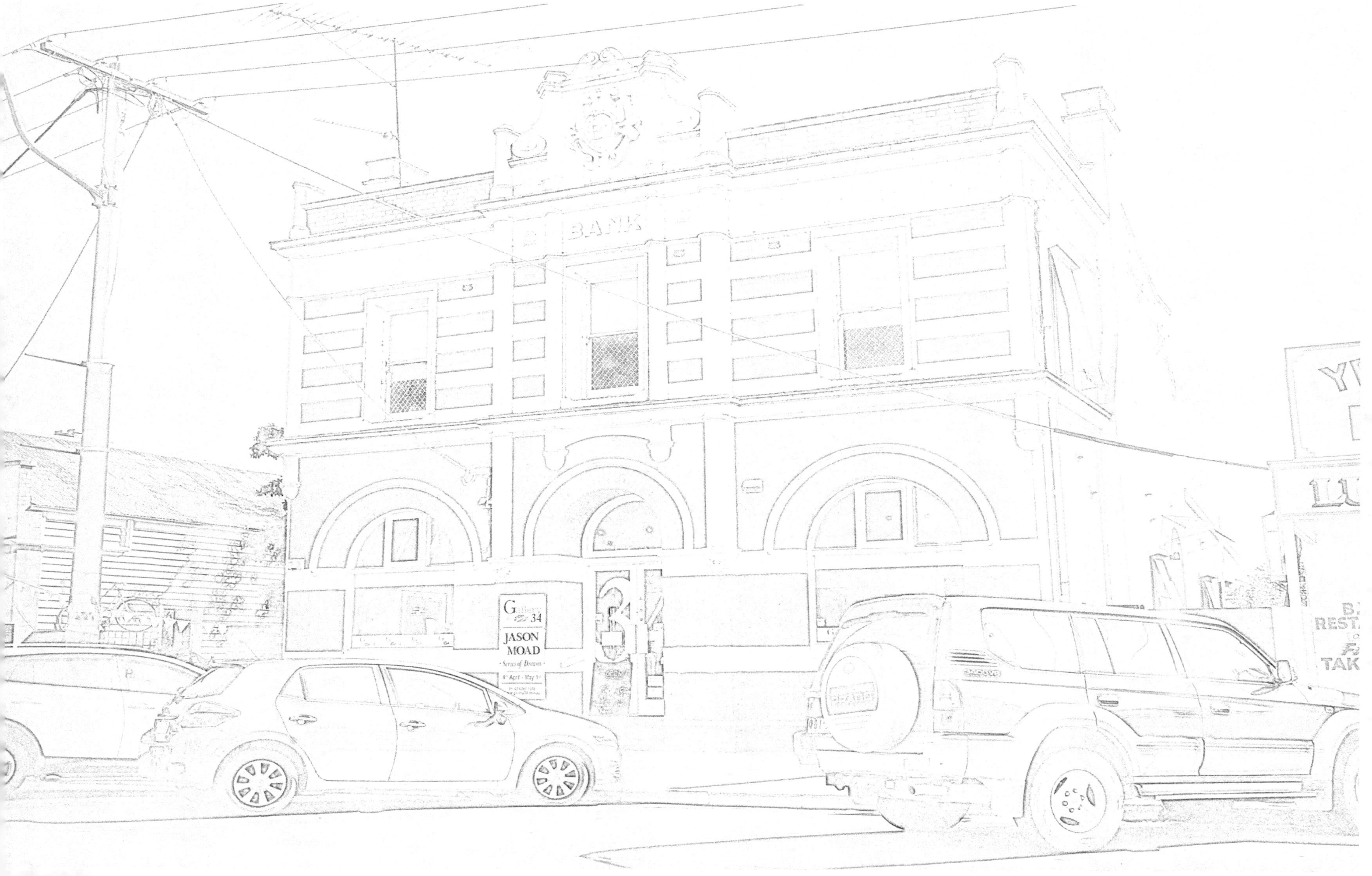
BANK
Gallery 34
JASON
MOAD
Series of Dreams

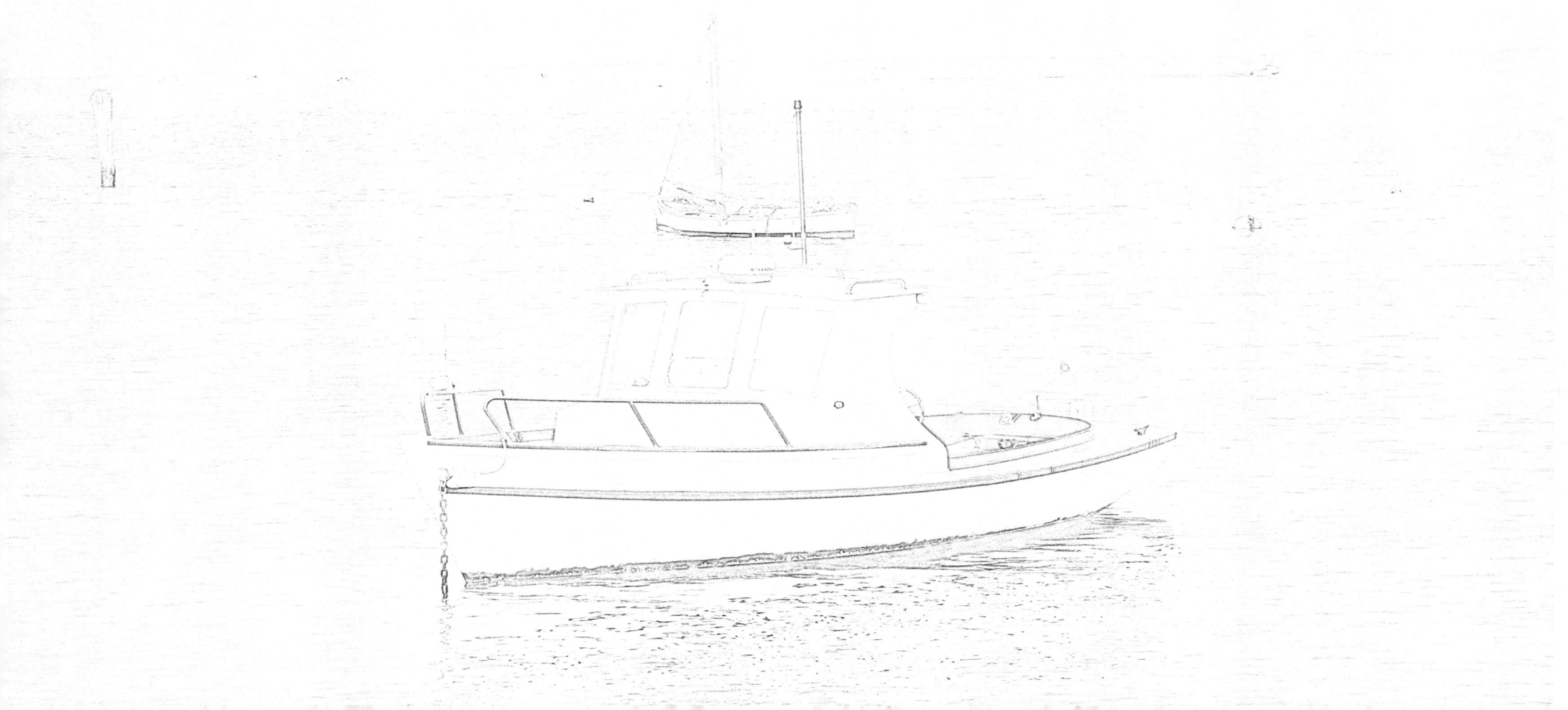

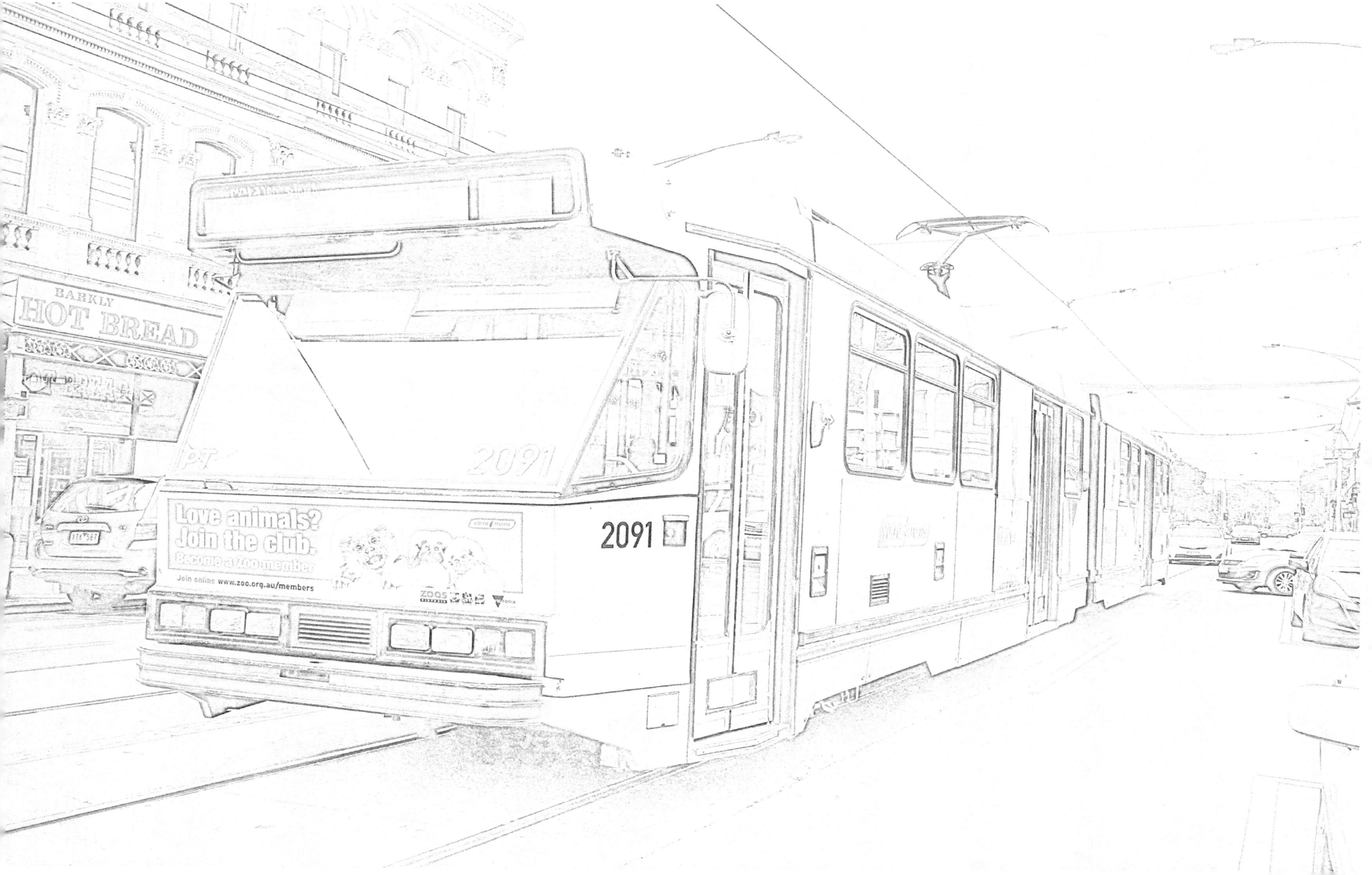
BARKLY
HOT BREAD
Love animals?
Join the club.
Become a zoo member
Join online www.zoo.org.au/members
2091
2091

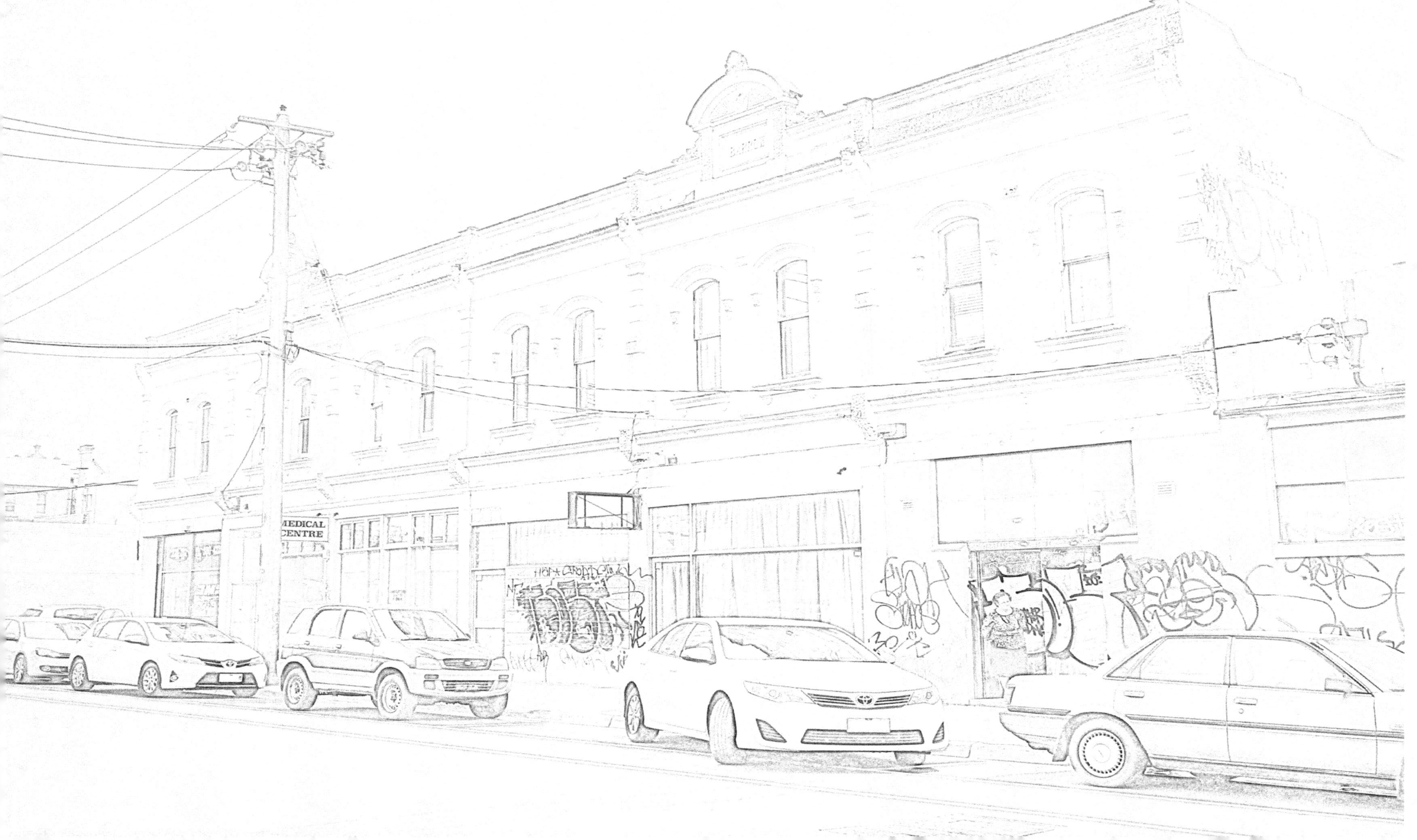
MEDICAL
CENTRE

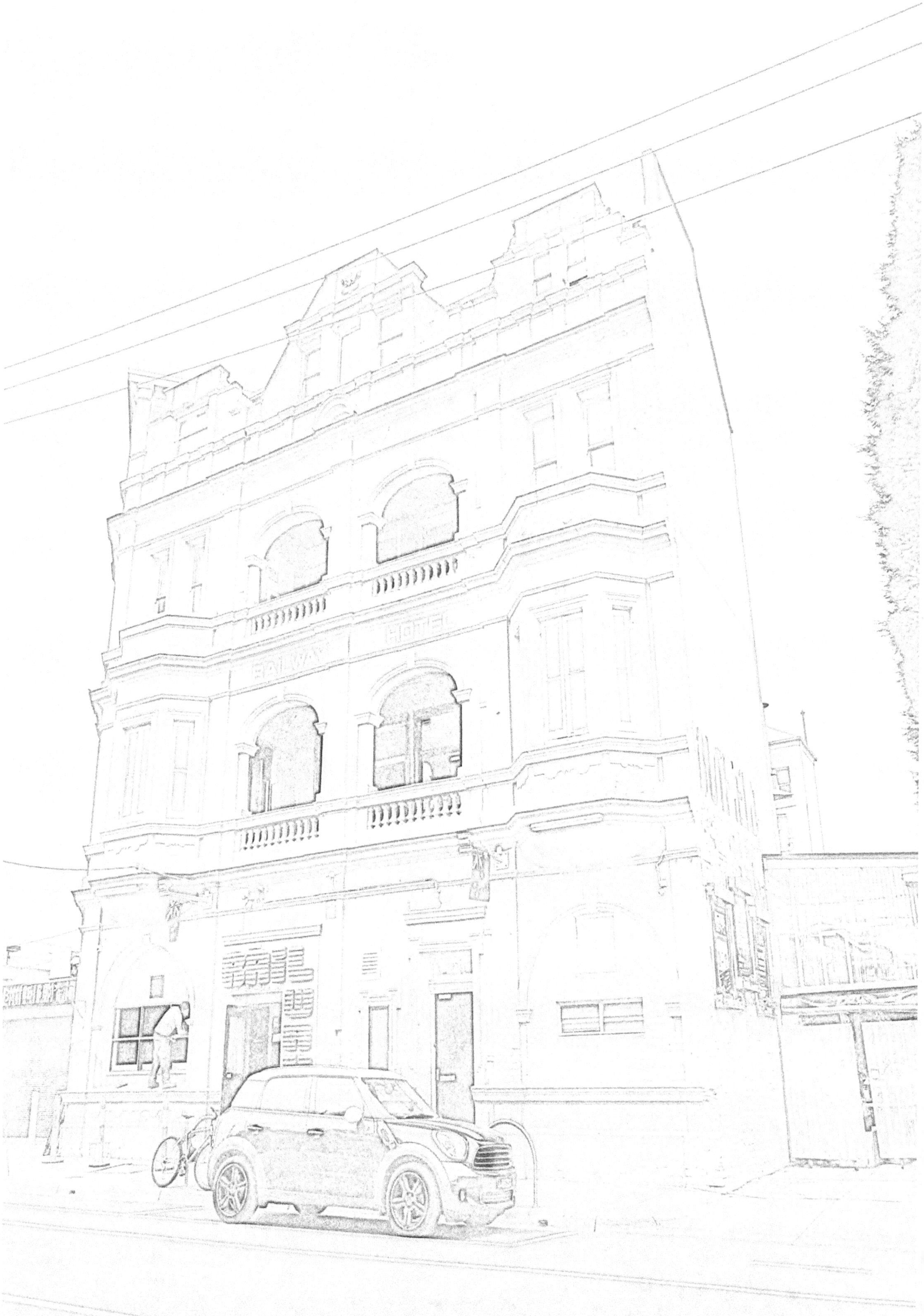

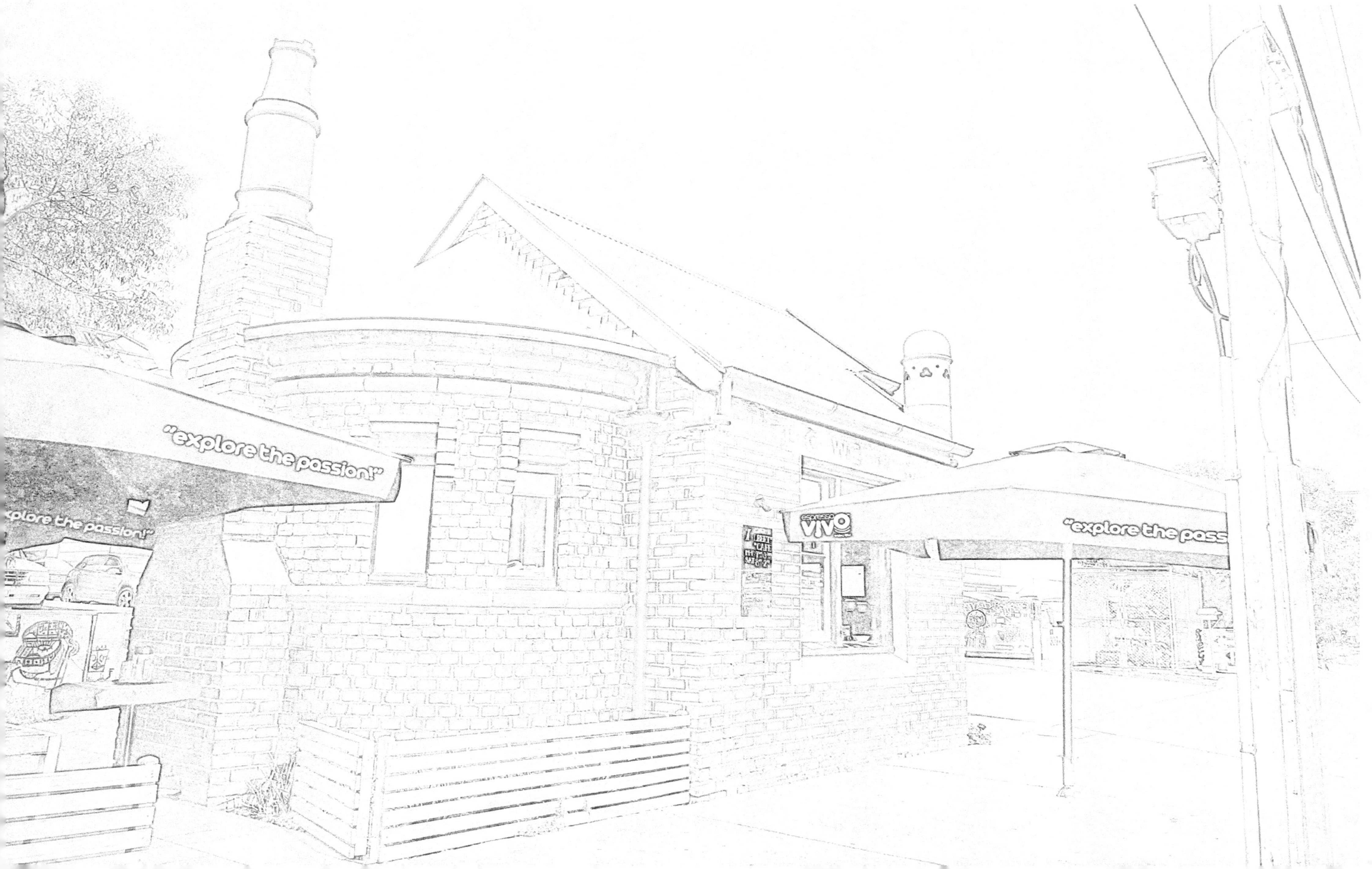
"explore the passion!"
xplore the passion!"
espresso
VIVO
"explore the pass

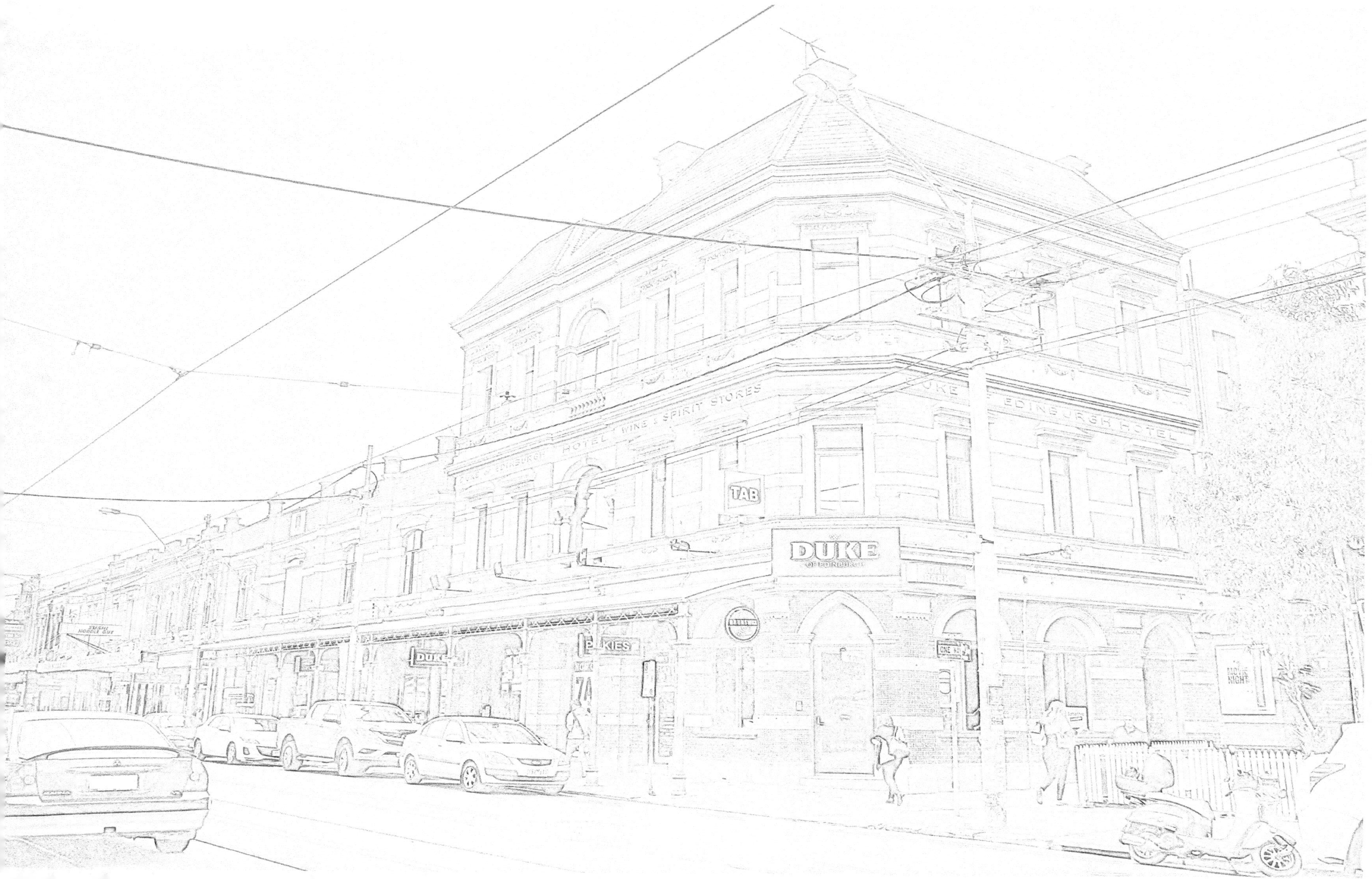

HOTEL WINE & SPIRIT STORES
EDINBURGH HOTEL
TAB
DUKE
OF EDINBURGH
DUKE
KIES
ONE WAY
MOVIE NIGHT
SUSHI NOODLE BAR

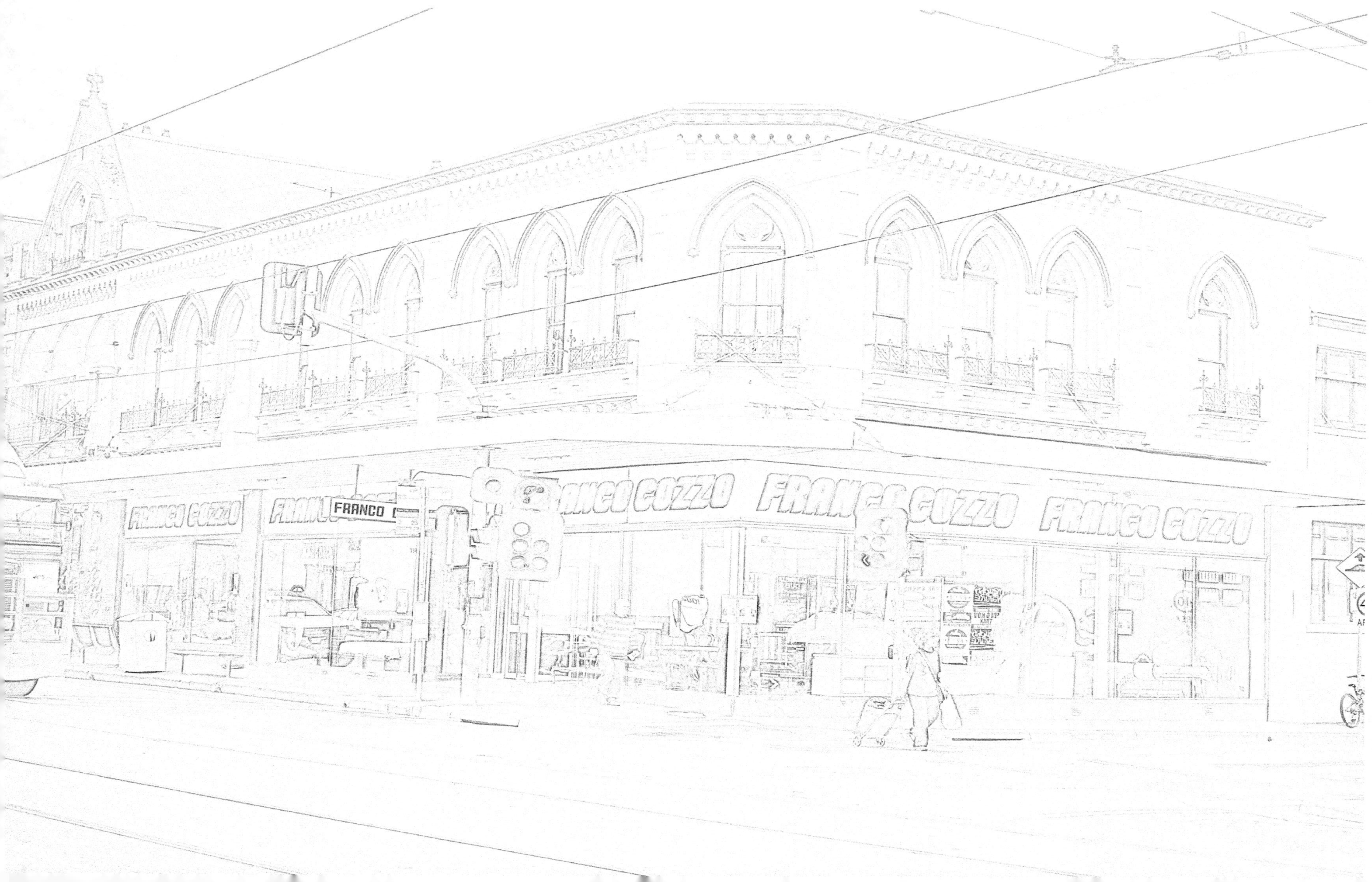
FRANCO GOZZO
FRANCO
FRANCO GOZZO
FRANCO GOZZO

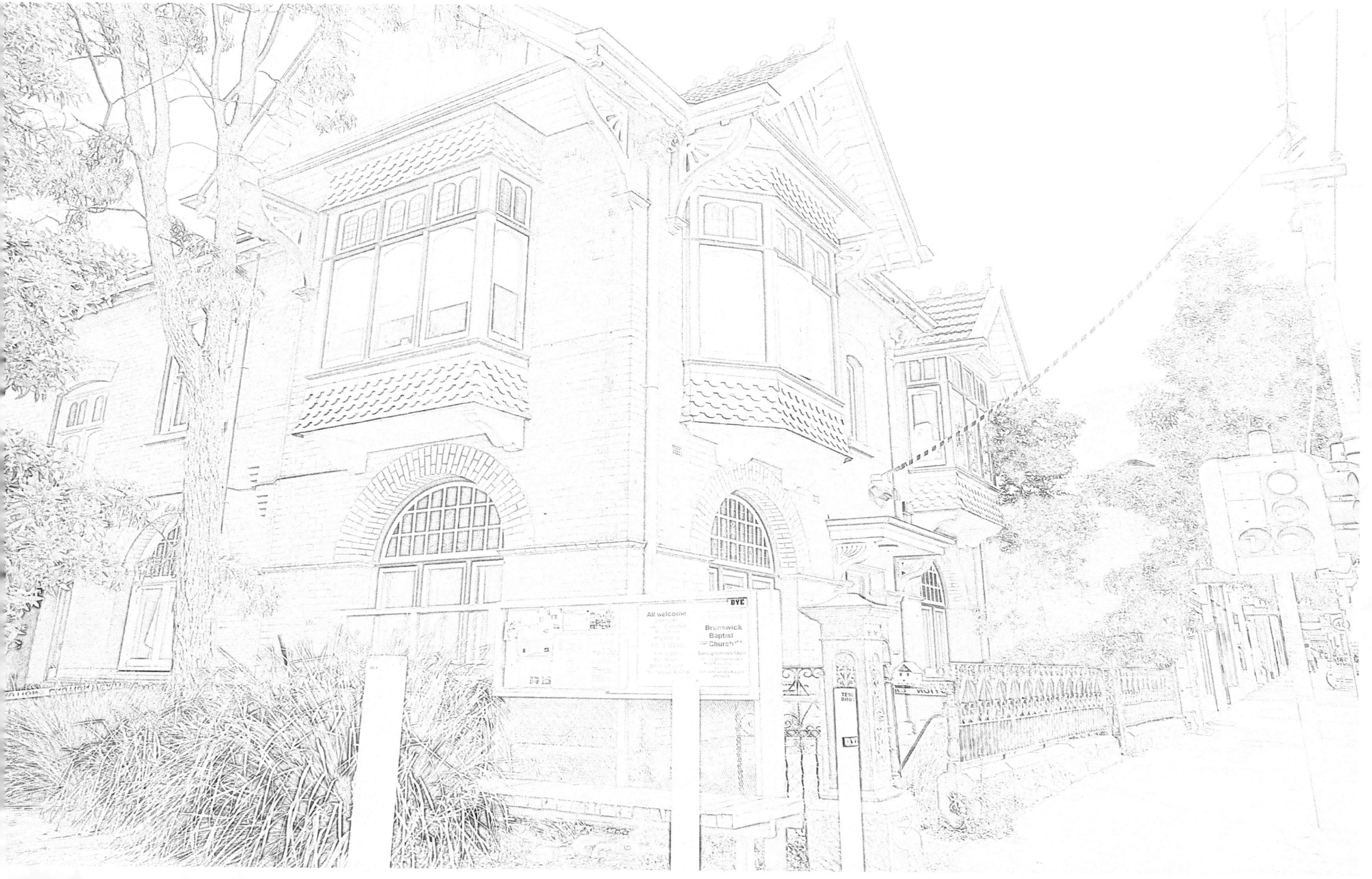

DYE
All welcome
Brunswick
Baptist
Church

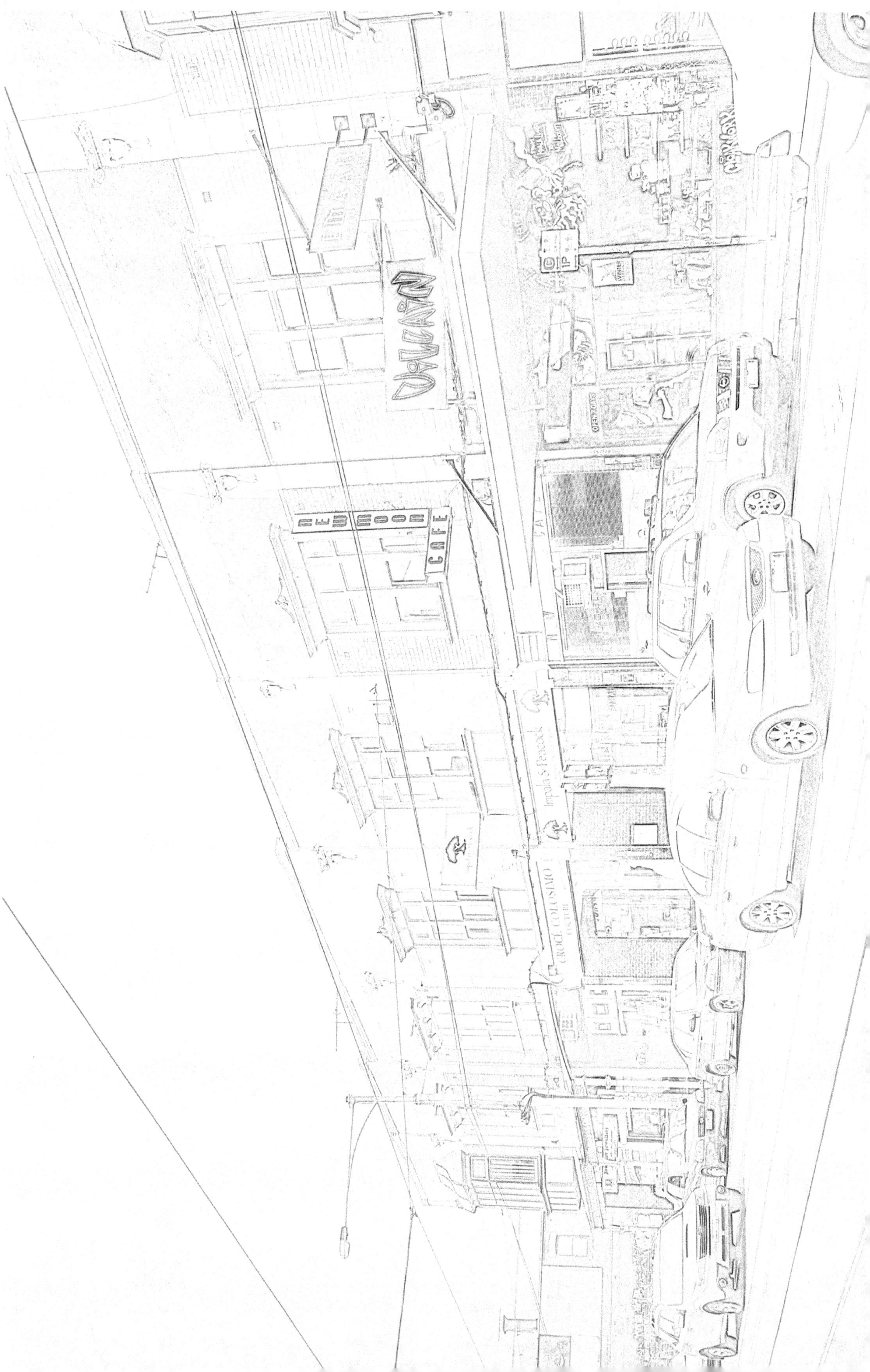
CAFE
Impala & Peacock
CROCE COLOSIMO

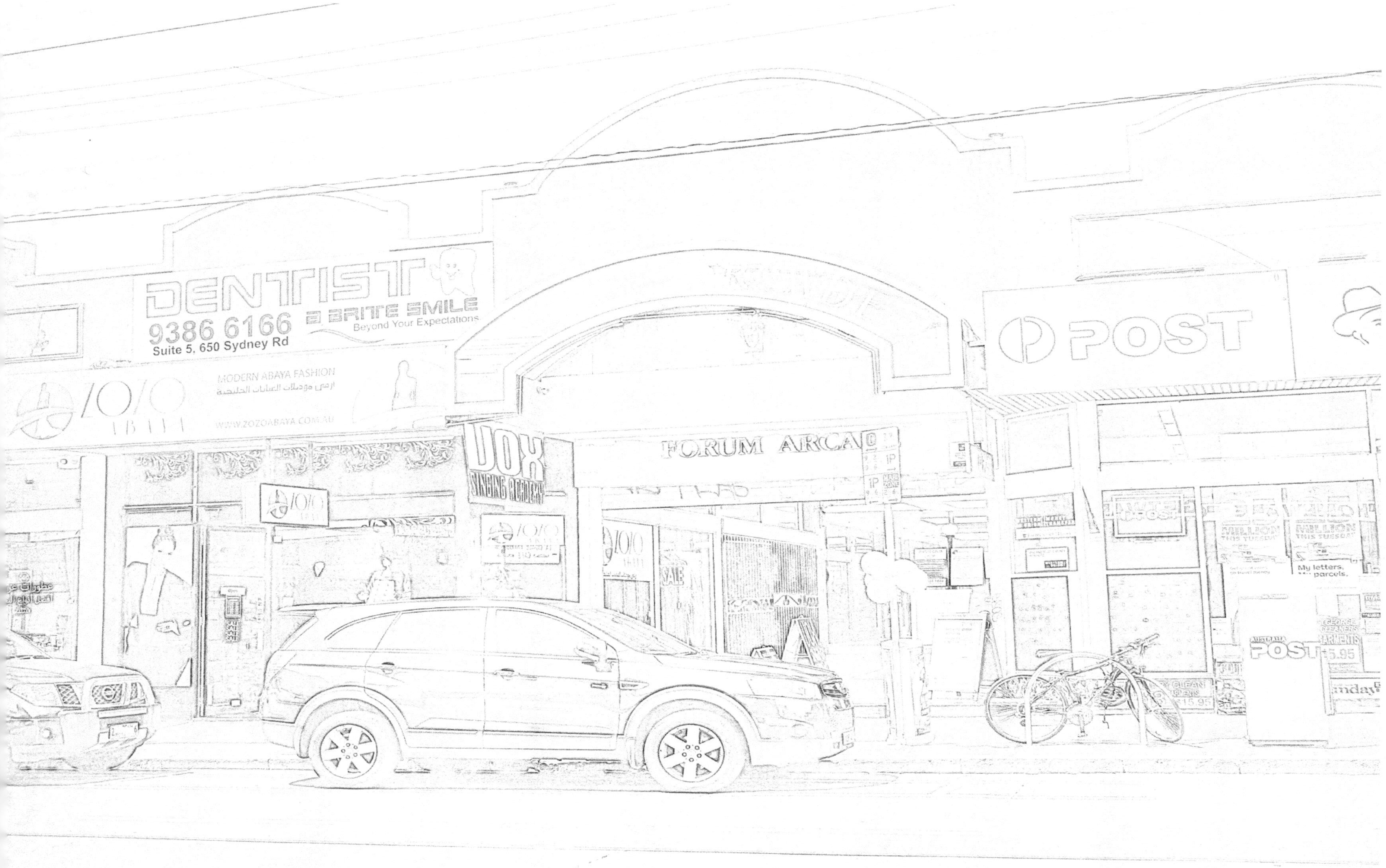
DENTIST
9386 6166
Suite 5, 650 Sydney Rd
a BRITE SMILE
Beyond Your Expectations
MODERN ABAYA FASHION
WWW.ZOZOABAYA.COM.AU
VOX
SINGING ACADEMY
FORUM ARCA
SALE
POST
MILLION
THIS TUESDAY
My letters,
parcels.
AUSTRALIA POST
GEORGE CLEANERS
$15.95

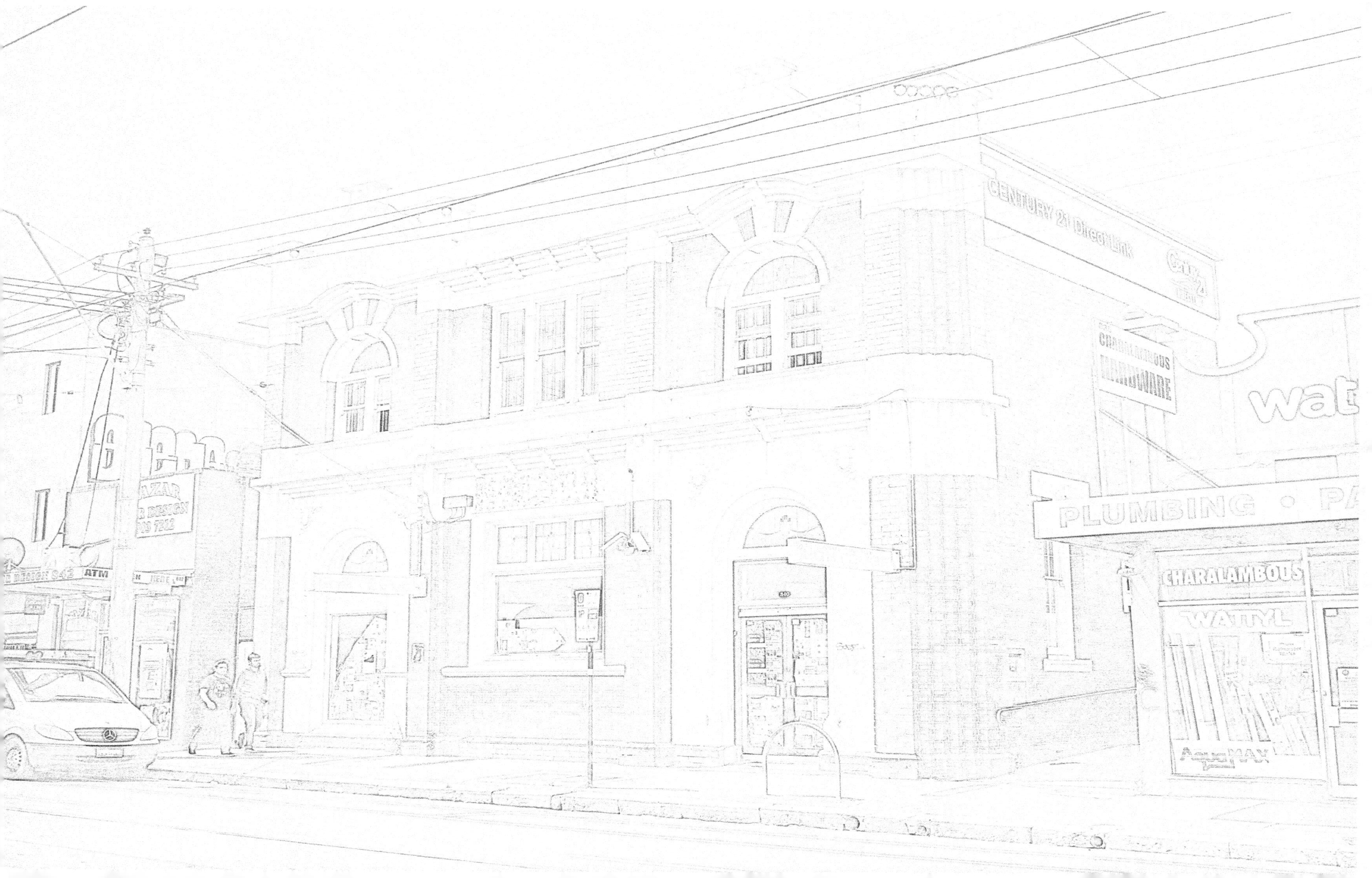
CENTURY 21 DirectLink
CHARALAMBOUS
HARDWARE
PLUMBING •
CHARALAMBOUS
WATTYL
ATM

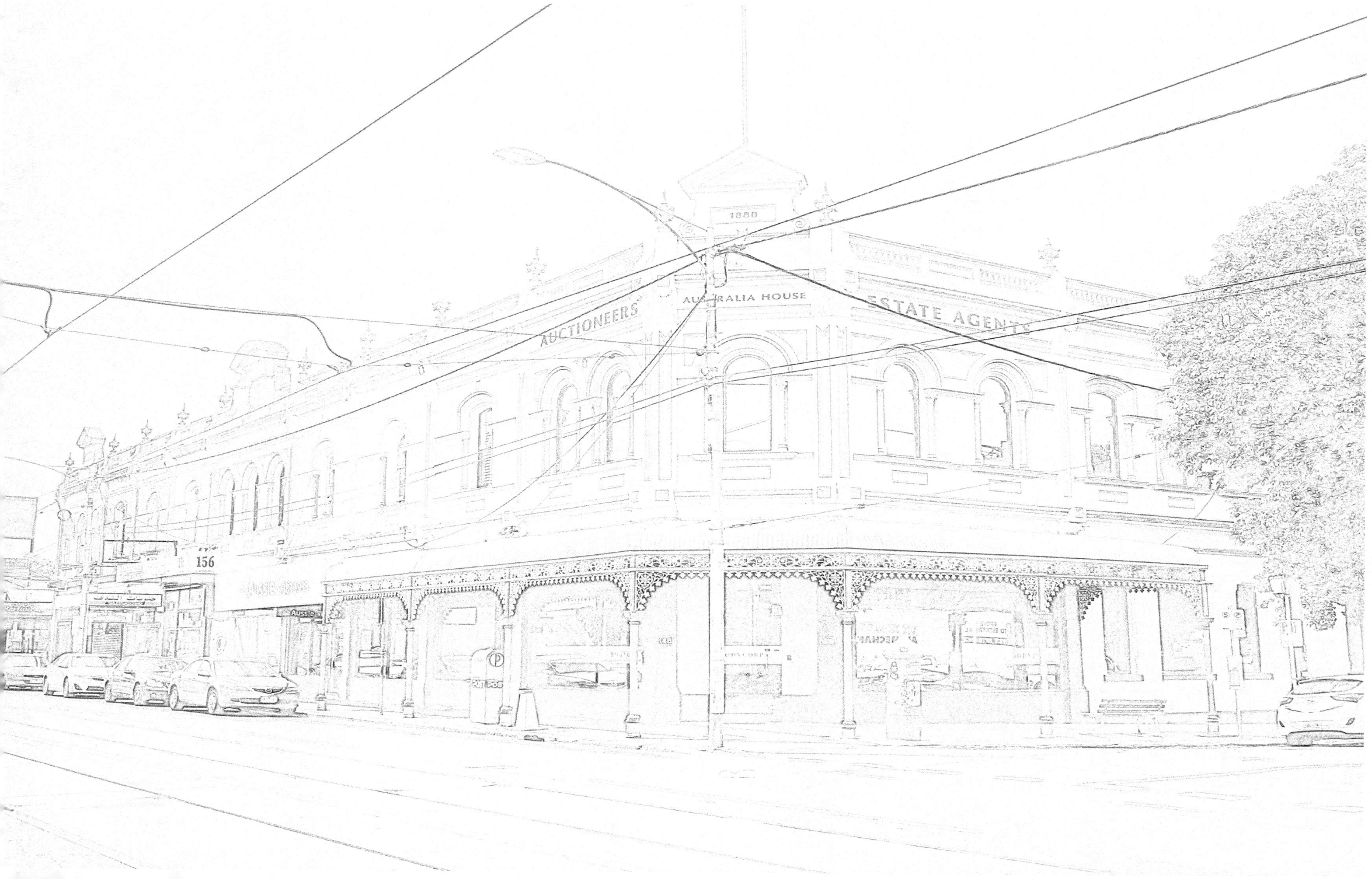
1888
AUSTRALIA HOUSE
AUCTIONEERS
ESTATE AGENTS
156
Aussie

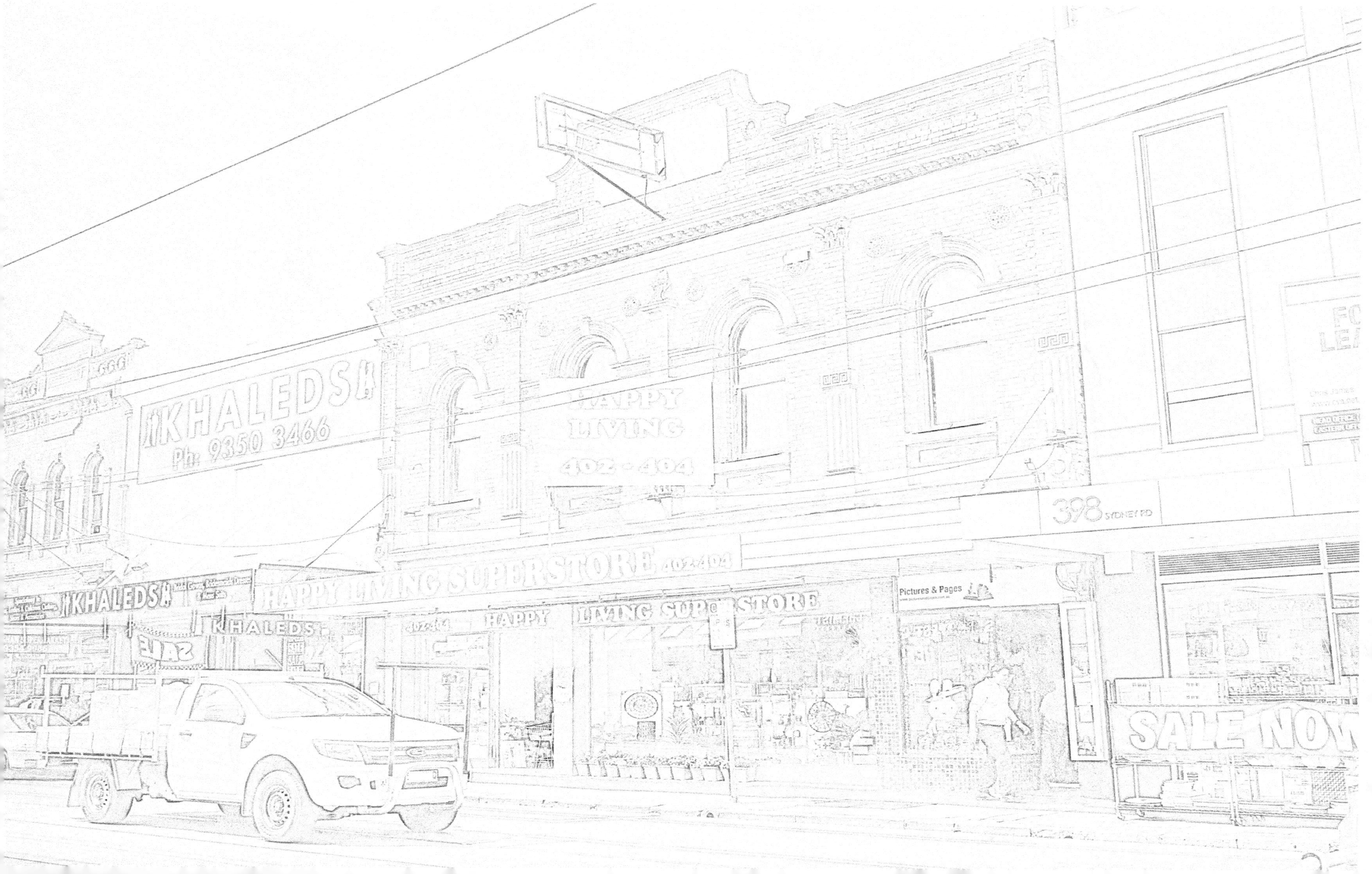
KHALEDS
Ph: 9350 3466
HAPPY
LIVING
402 - 404
398 SYDNEY RD
HAPPY LIVING SUPERSTORE 402-404
HAPPY
LIVING SUPERSTORE
KHALEDS
Pictures & Pages
SALE NOW

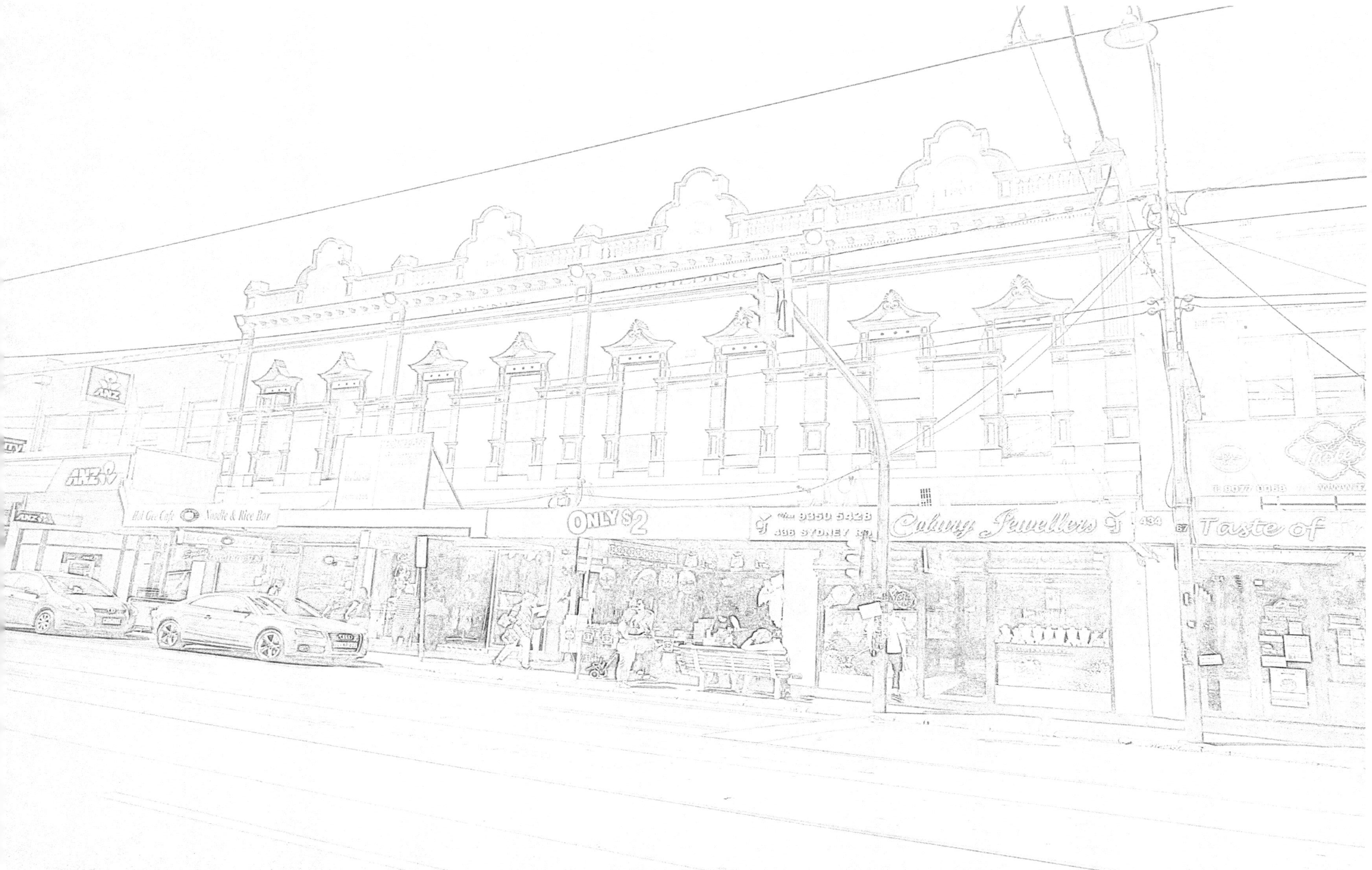
ANZ
Noodle & Rice Bar
ONLY $2
434
Taste of

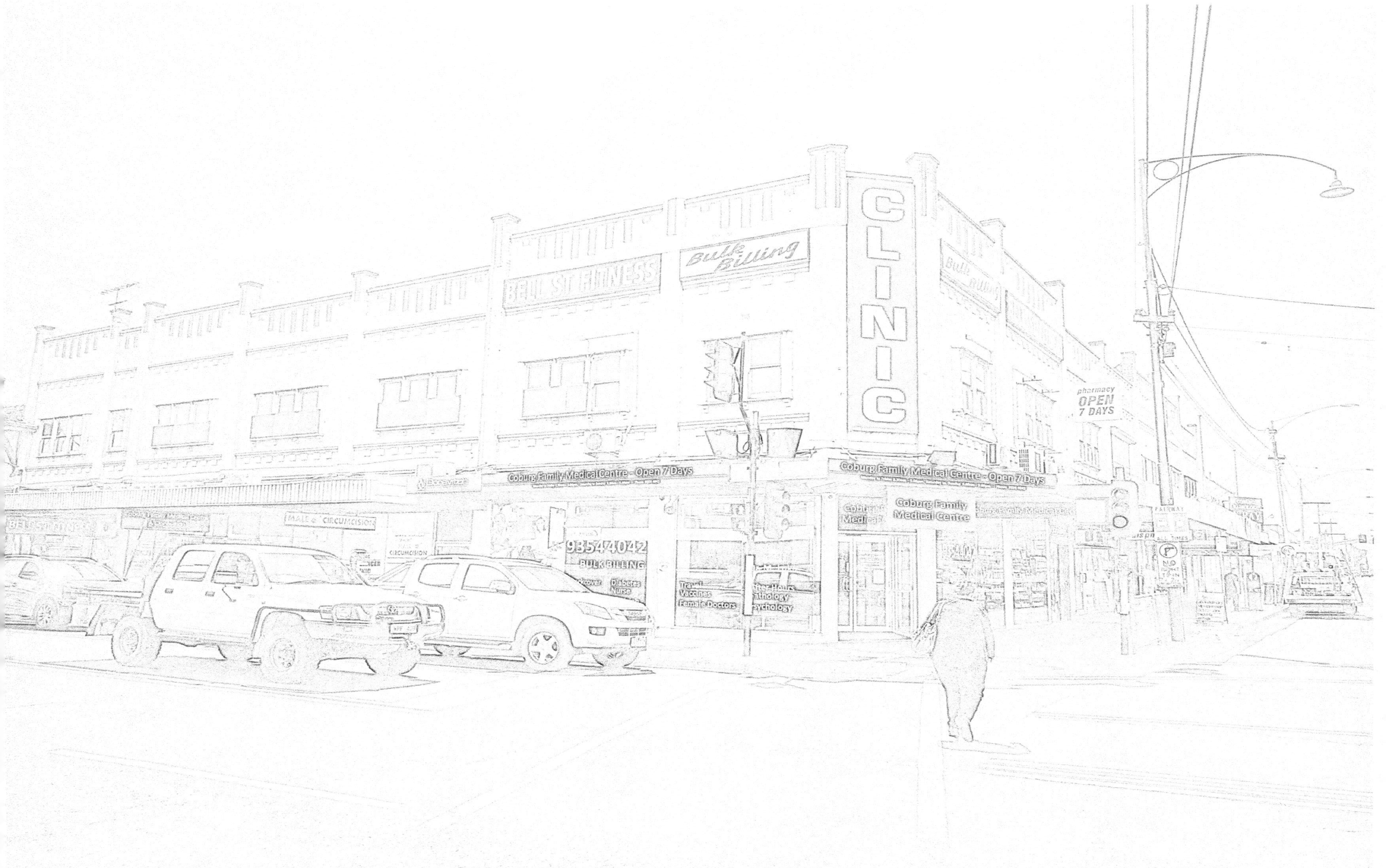
CLINIC
Bulk Billing
BELL ST FITNESS
pharmacy OPEN 7 DAYS
Coburg Family Medical Centre - Open 7 Days
Coburg Family Medical Centre - Open 7 Days
Coburg Family Medical Centre
93544042
BULK BILLING
Diabetes Nurse
Travel Vaccines Female Doctors
MALE CIRCUMCISION

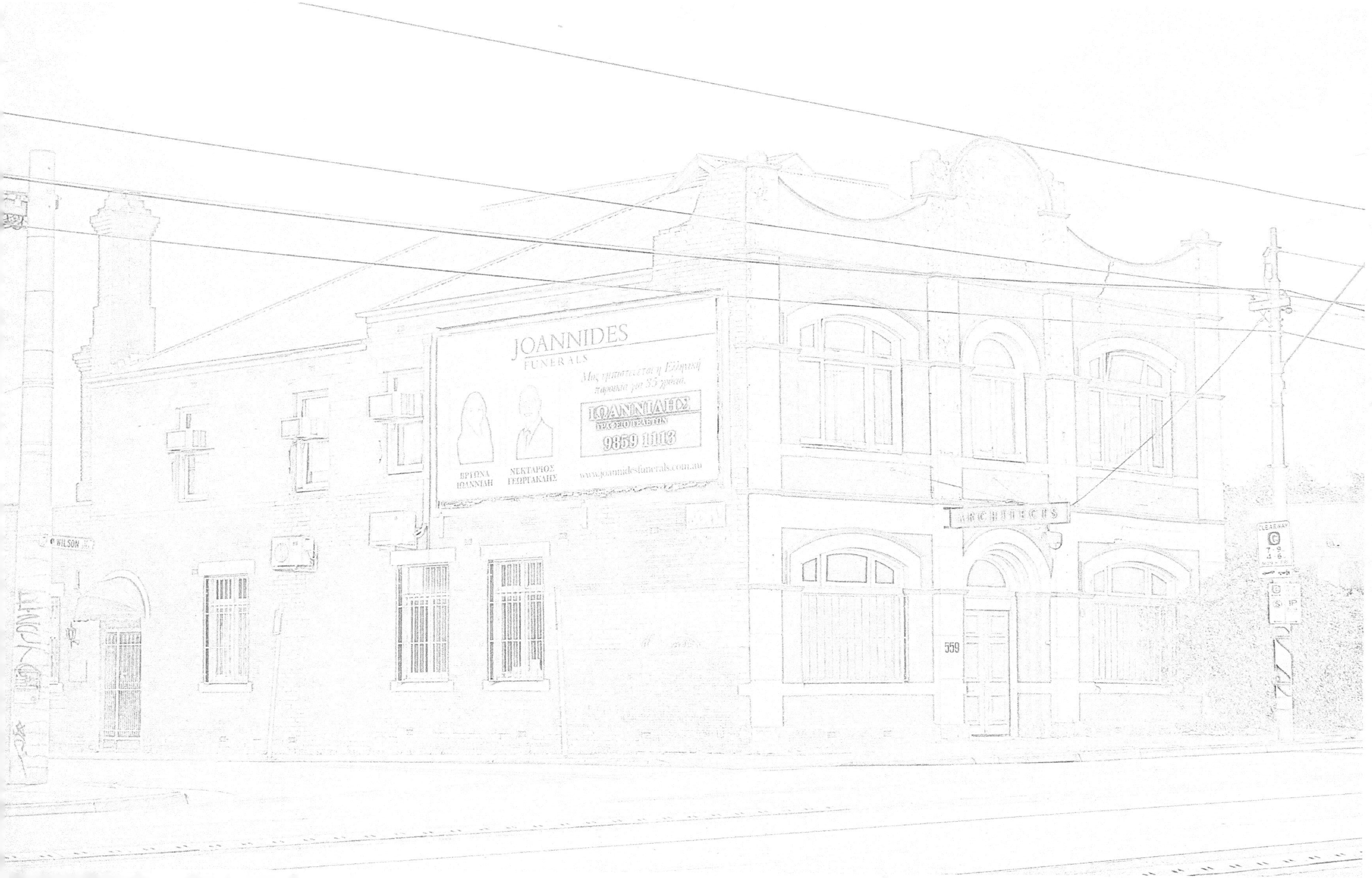

JOANNIDES
FUNERALS
ΙΩΑΝΝΙΔΗΣ
9859 1113
www.joannidesfunerals.com.au
ARCHITECTS
559
WILSON
CLEARWAY

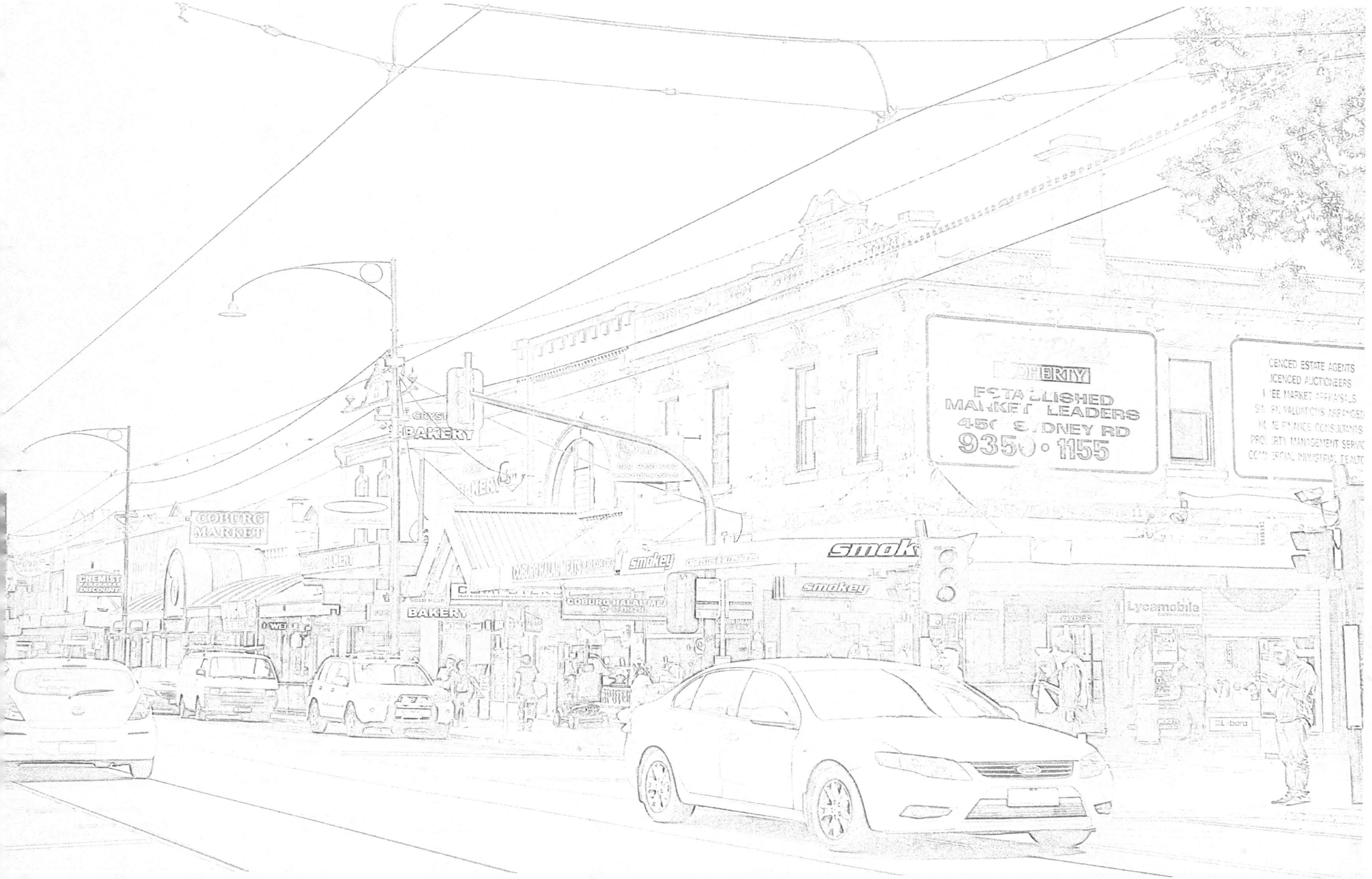
ESTABLISHED
MARKET LEADERS
9350 • 1155
COBURG
MARKET
CHEMIST
DISCOUNT
BAKERY
BAKERY
smokey
smokey
COBURG HALAL MEATS
Lycamobile

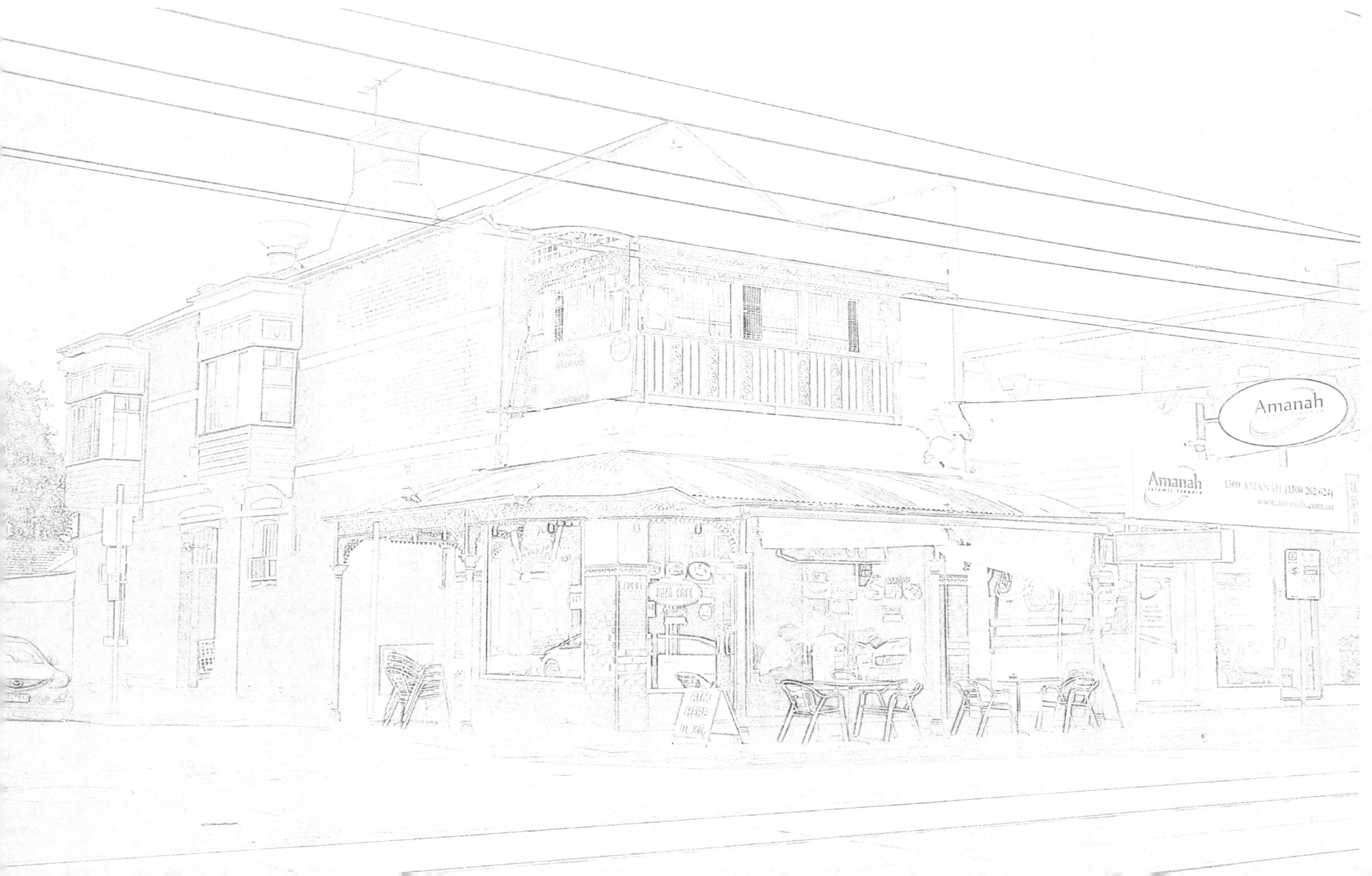
Amanah
Amanah
1300 AMANAH (1300 262 624)
ATM
HERE

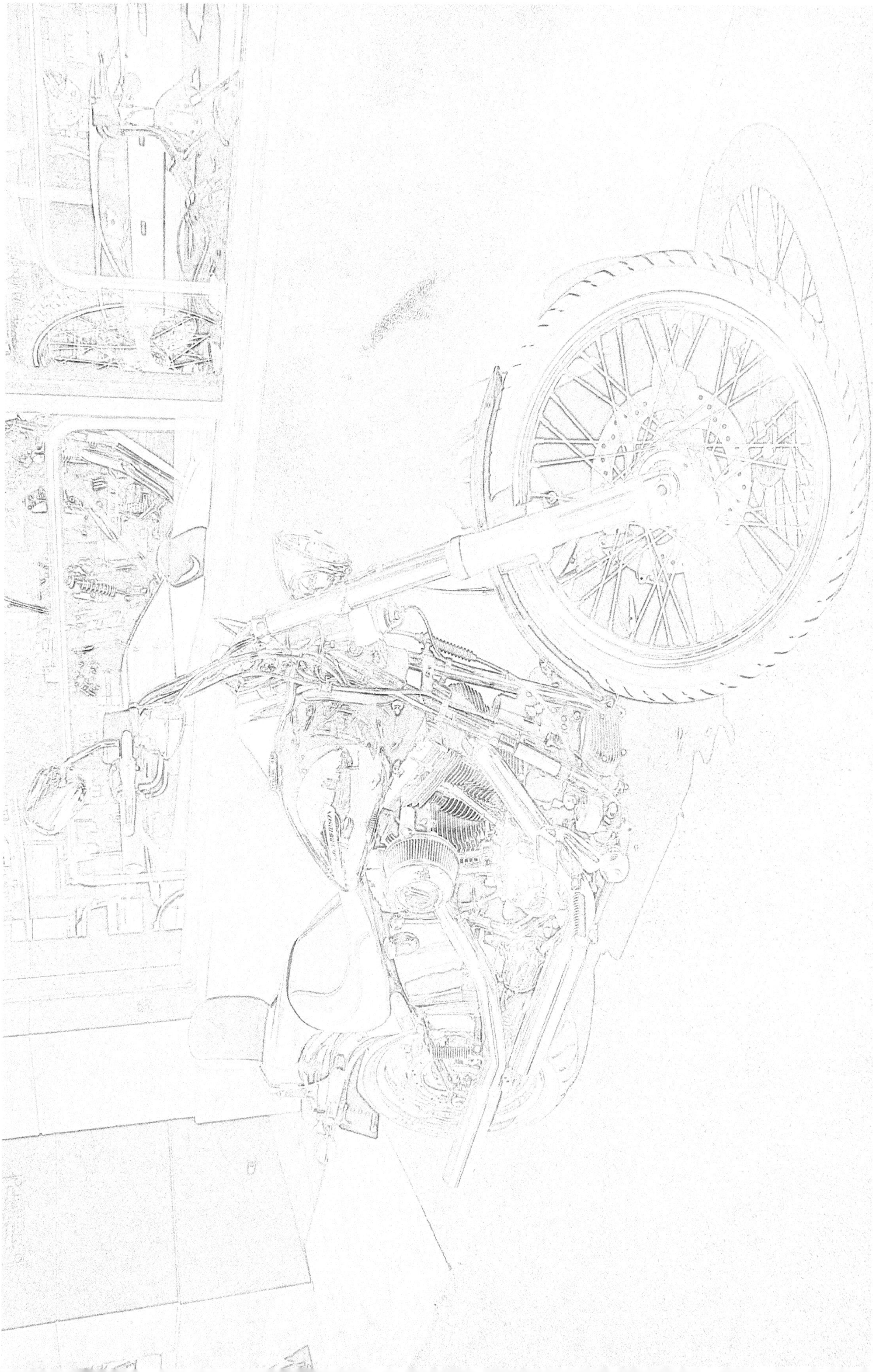

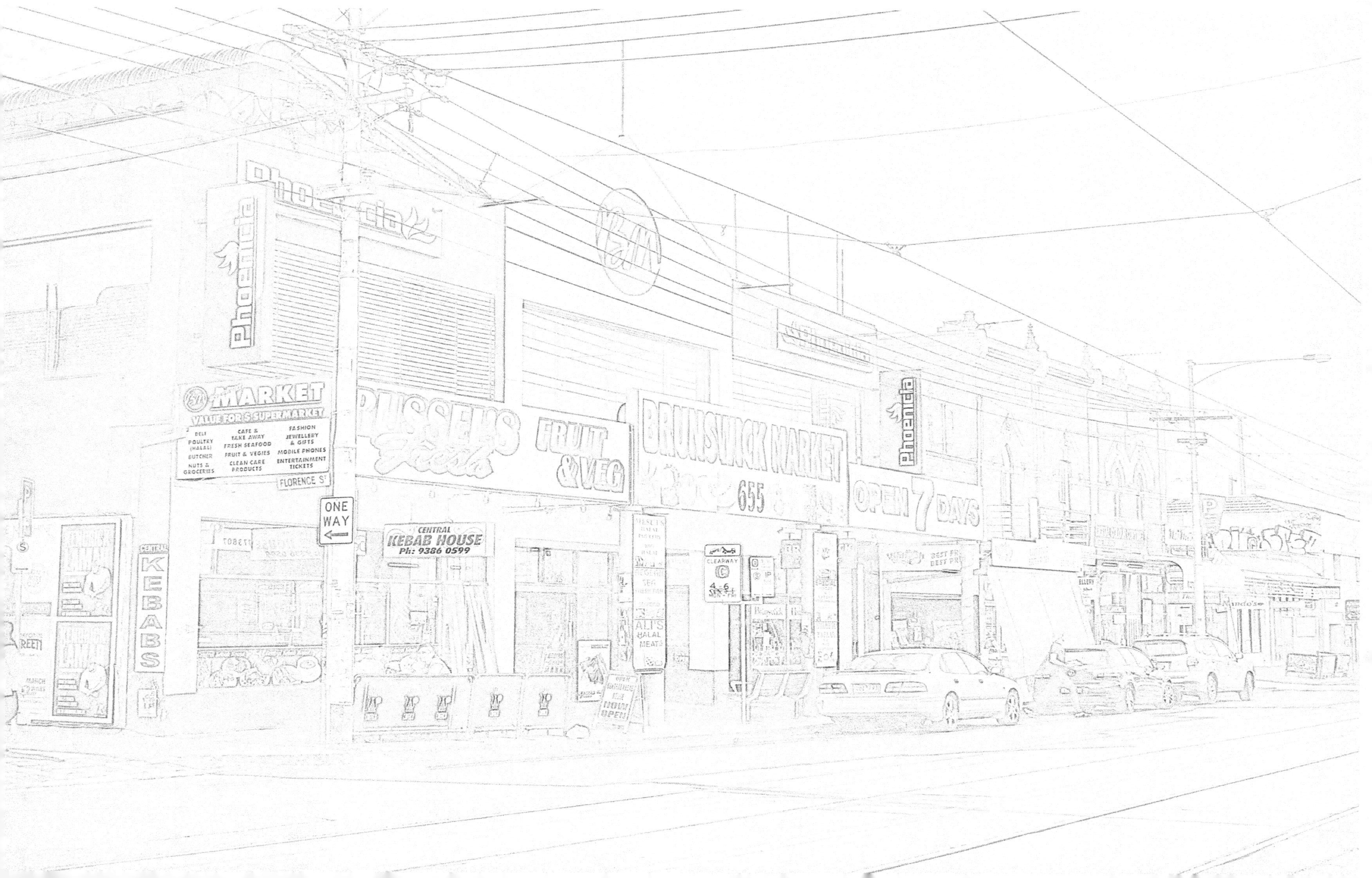
Phoenicia
MARKET
VALUE FOR $ SUPERMARKET
DELI
POULTRY (HALAL)
BUTCHER
NUTS & GROCERIES
CAFE & TAKE AWAY
FRESH SEAFOOD
FRUIT & VEGIES
CLEAN CARE PRODUCTS
FASHION
JEWELLERY & GIFTS
MOBILE PHONES
ENTERTAINMENT TICKETS
FLORENCE ST
ONE WAY
CENTRAL
KEBAB HOUSE
Ph: 9386 0599
CENTRAL
KEBABS
FRUIT & VEG
BRUNSWICK MARKET
655
OPEN 7 DAYS
CLEARWAY
ALI'S
HALAL
MEATS
NOW OPEN

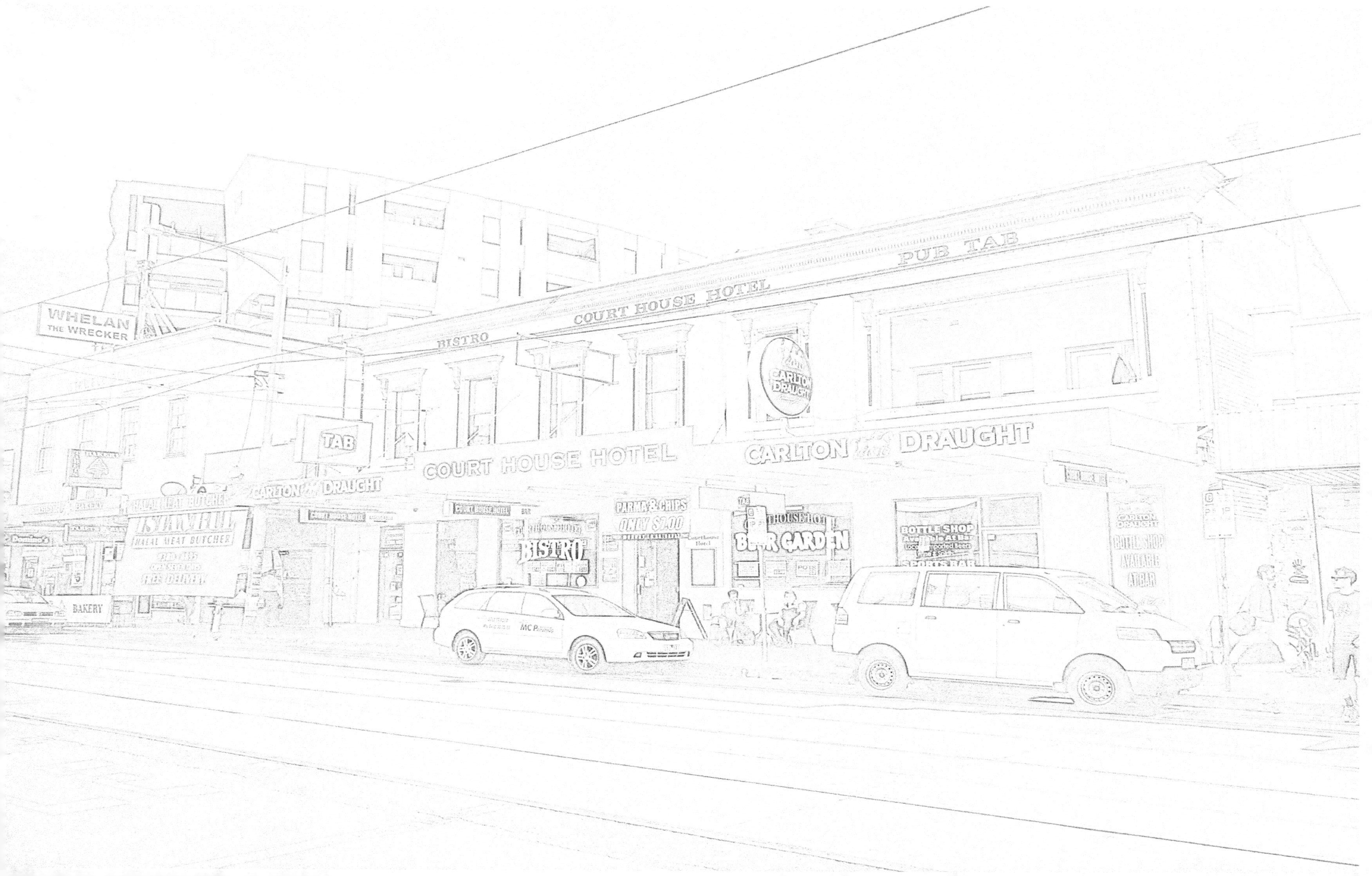
WHELAN
THE WRECKER
PUB TAB
COURT HOUSE HOTEL
BISTRO
CARLTON DRAUGHT
TAB
COURT HOUSE HOTEL
CARLTON DRAUGHT
CARLTON DRAUGHT
HALAL MEAT BUTCHER
FREE DELIVERY
BAKERY
PARMA & CHIPS
ONLY $7.00
BISTRO
BOTTLE SHOP
SPORTS BAR
BOTTLE SHOP
AVAILABLE
AT BAR
MC Parking

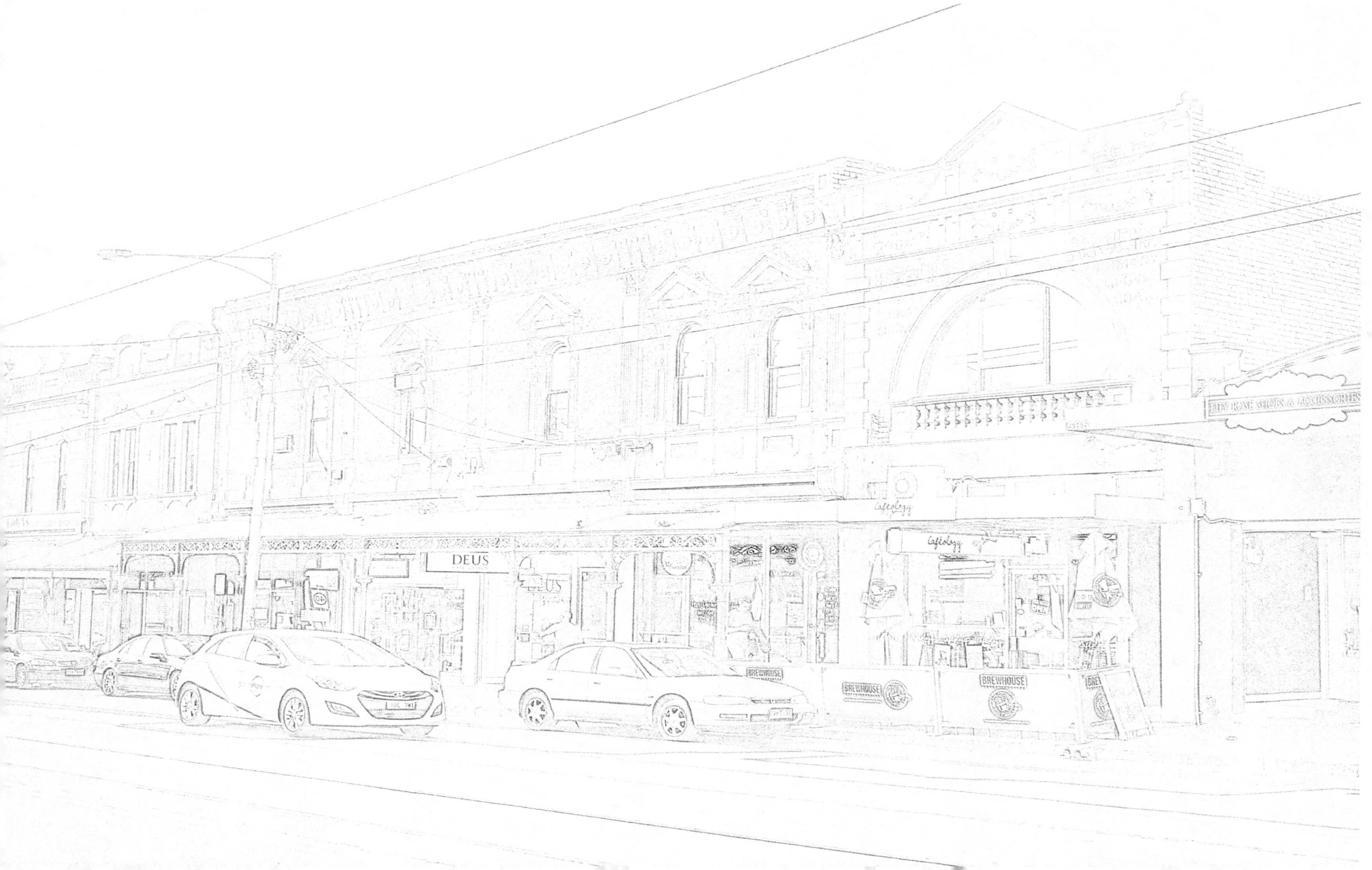
DEUS
Cafeology
BREWHOUSE
BREWHOUSE
BREWHOUSE

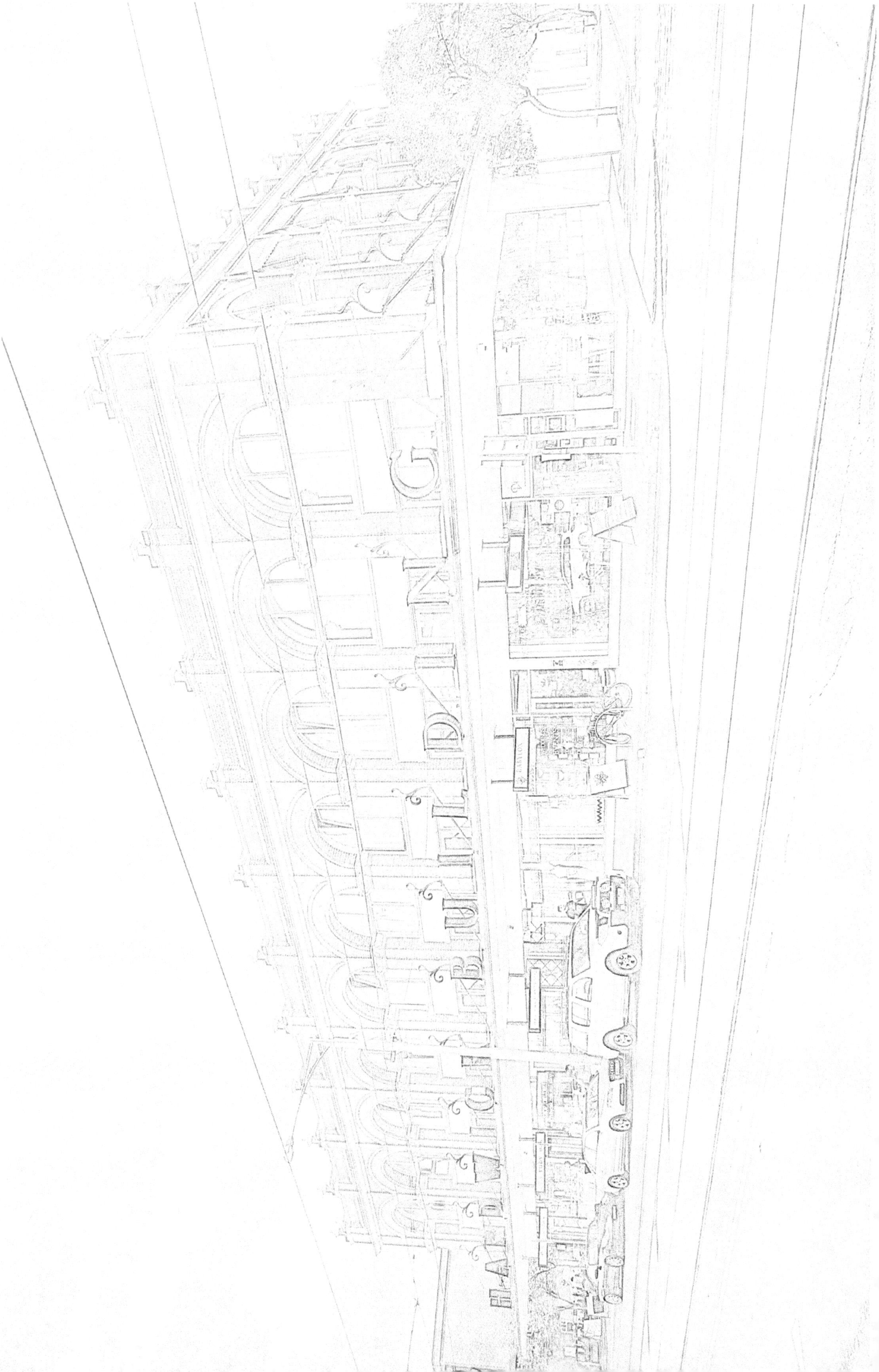

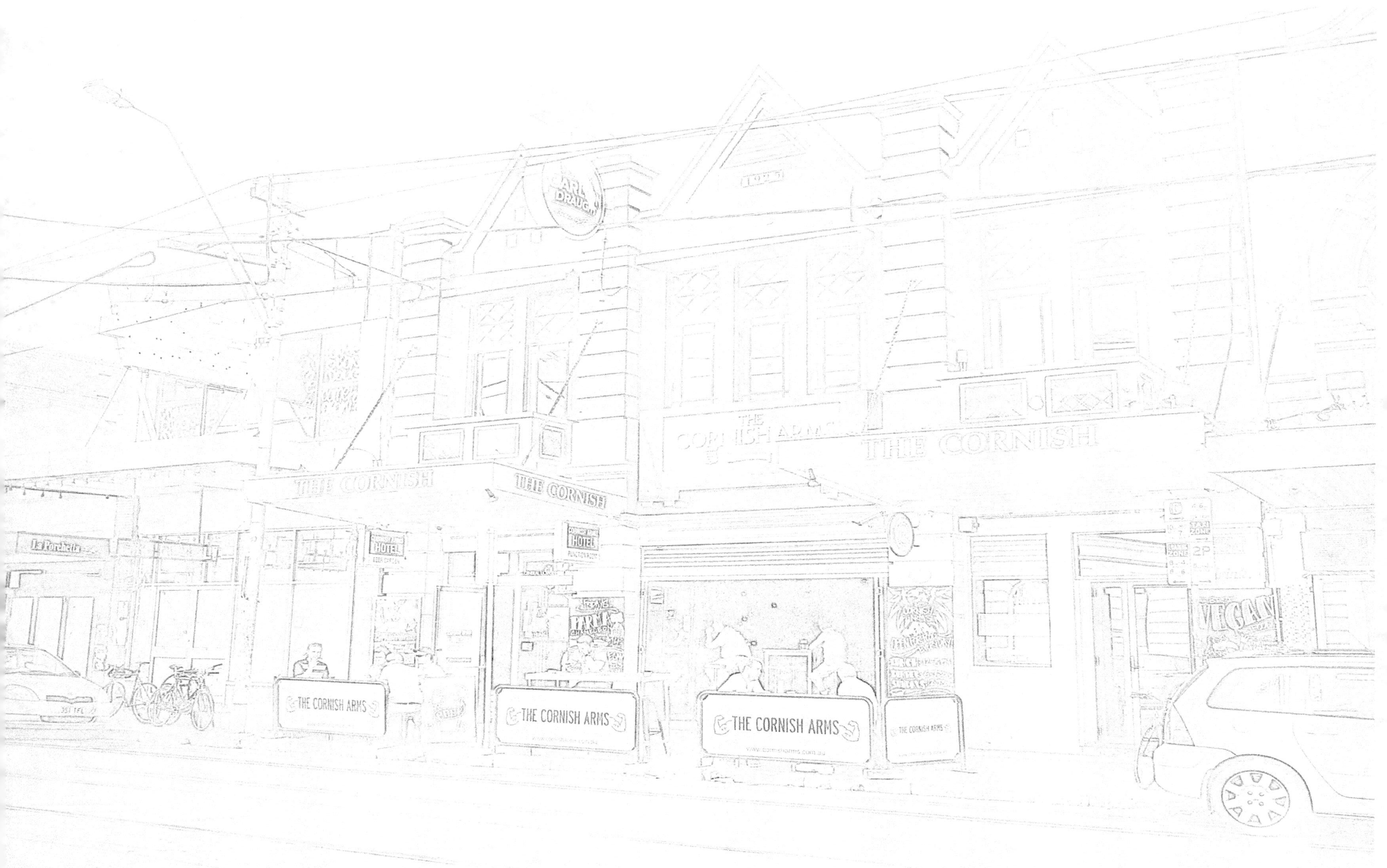
THE CORNISH
THE CORNISH
THE CORNISH
HOTEL
HOTEL
2P
VEGAN
La Porchetta
THE CORNISH ARMS
THE CORNISH ARMS
THE CORNISH ARMS
THE CORNISH ARMS

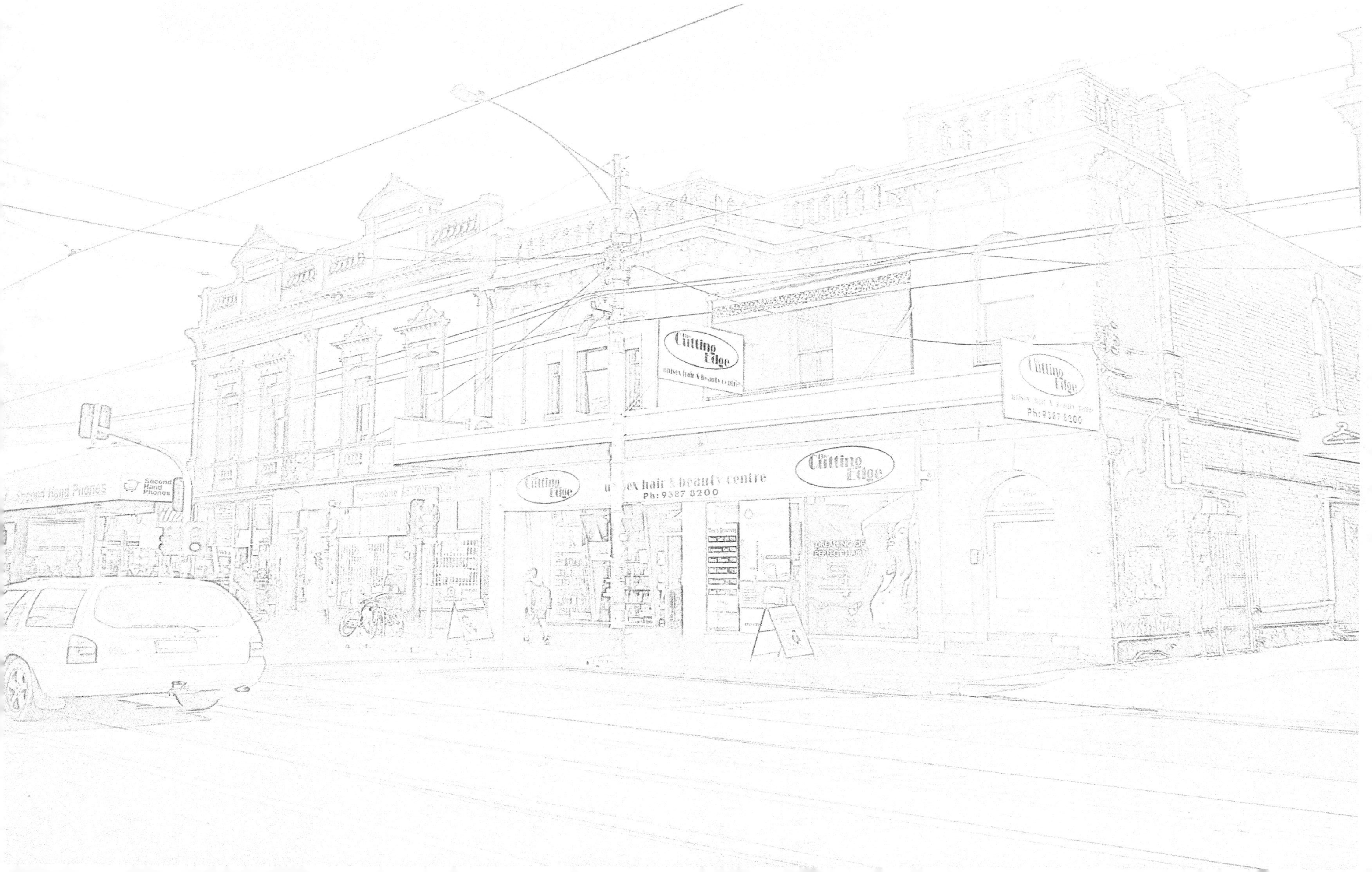
The Cutting Edge
unisex hair & beauty centre
Ph: 9387 8200
Second Hand Phones
Second Hand Phones
DREAMING OF PERFECT HAIR

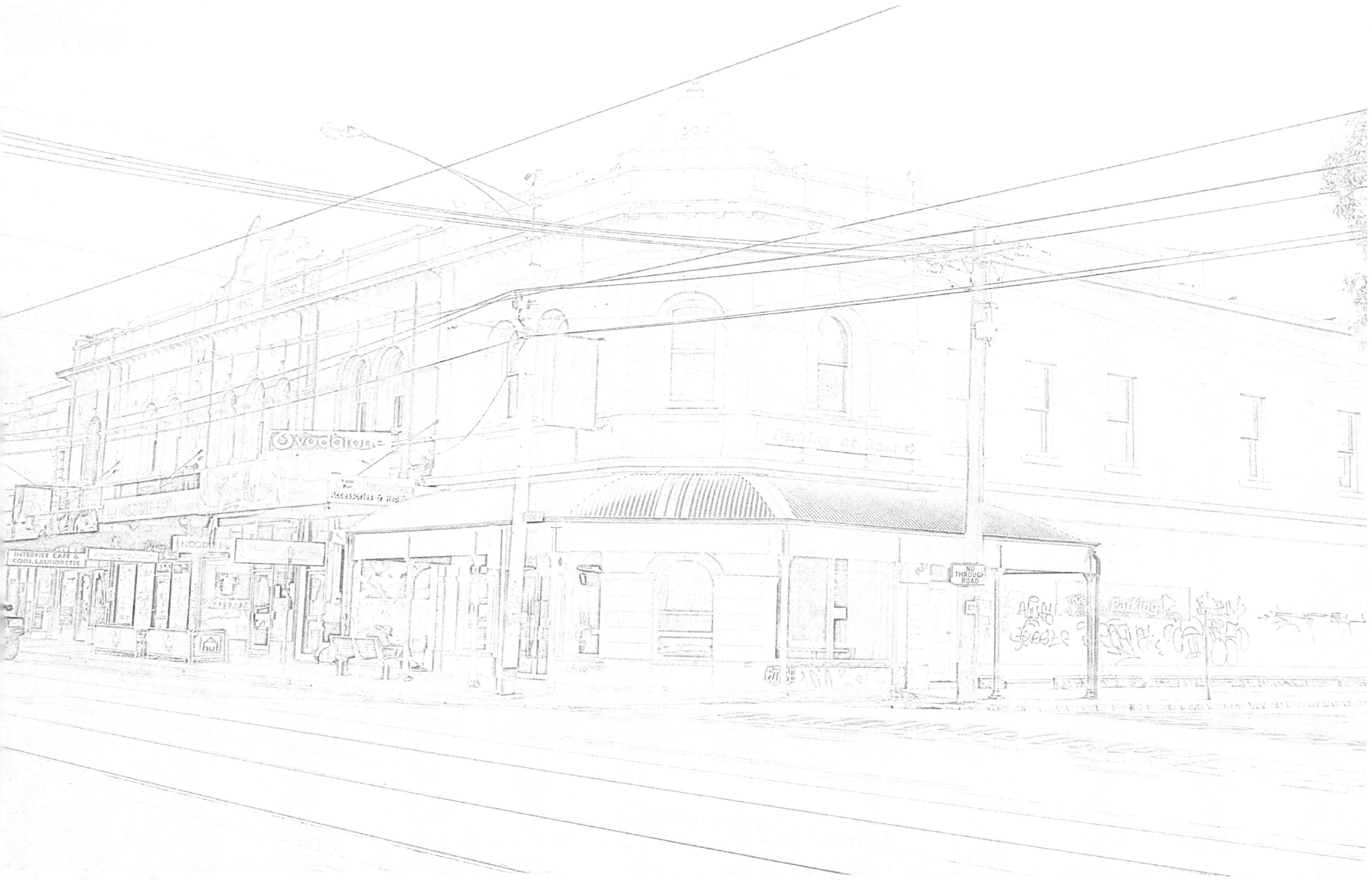

NO THROUGH ROAD
Vodafone
INTERNET CAFE &
COIN LAUNDRETTE

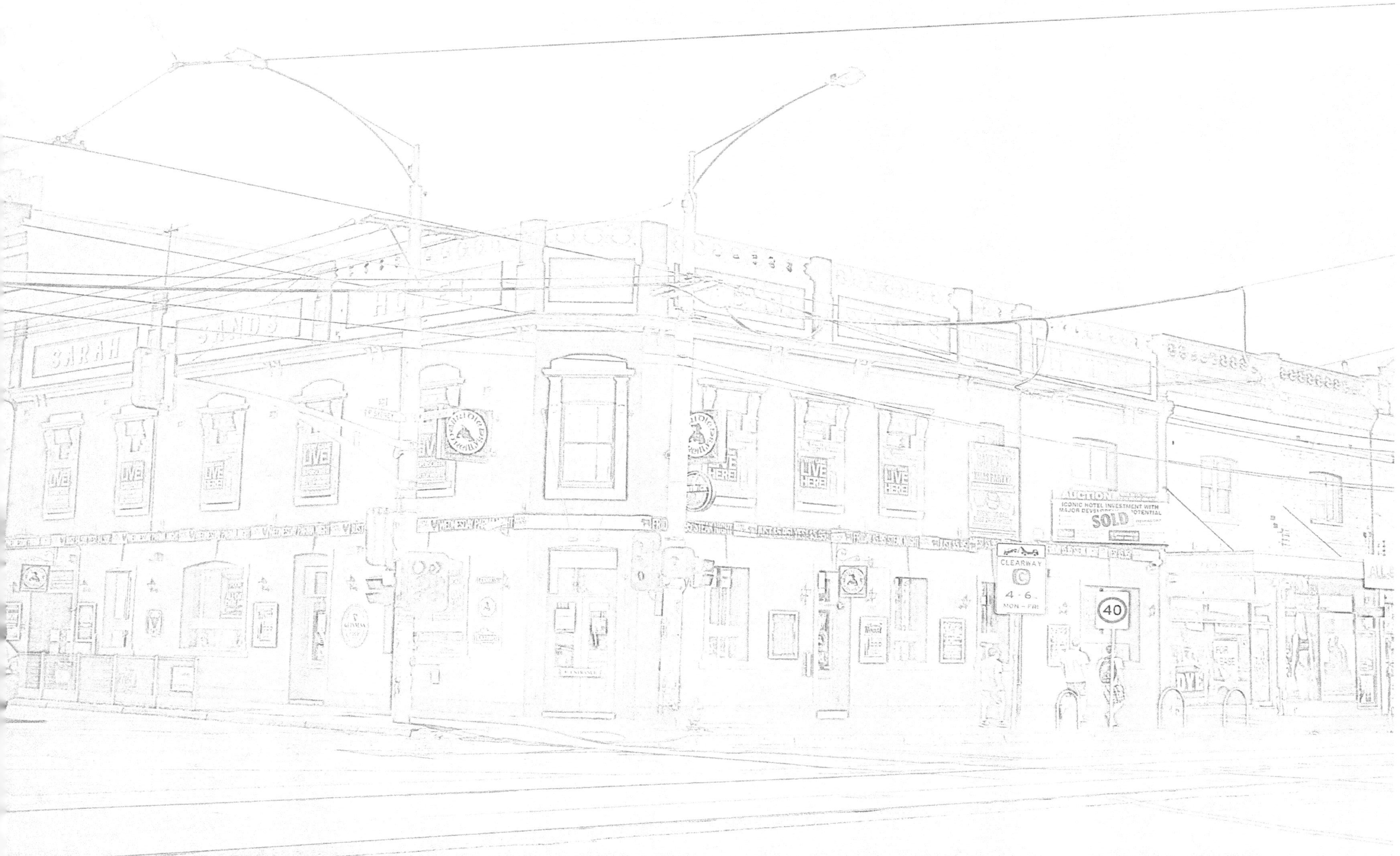

SARAH
SANDS
LIVE HERE
ICONIC HOTEL INVESTMENT WITH
SOLD
CLEARWAY
4 - 6
MON - FRI
40

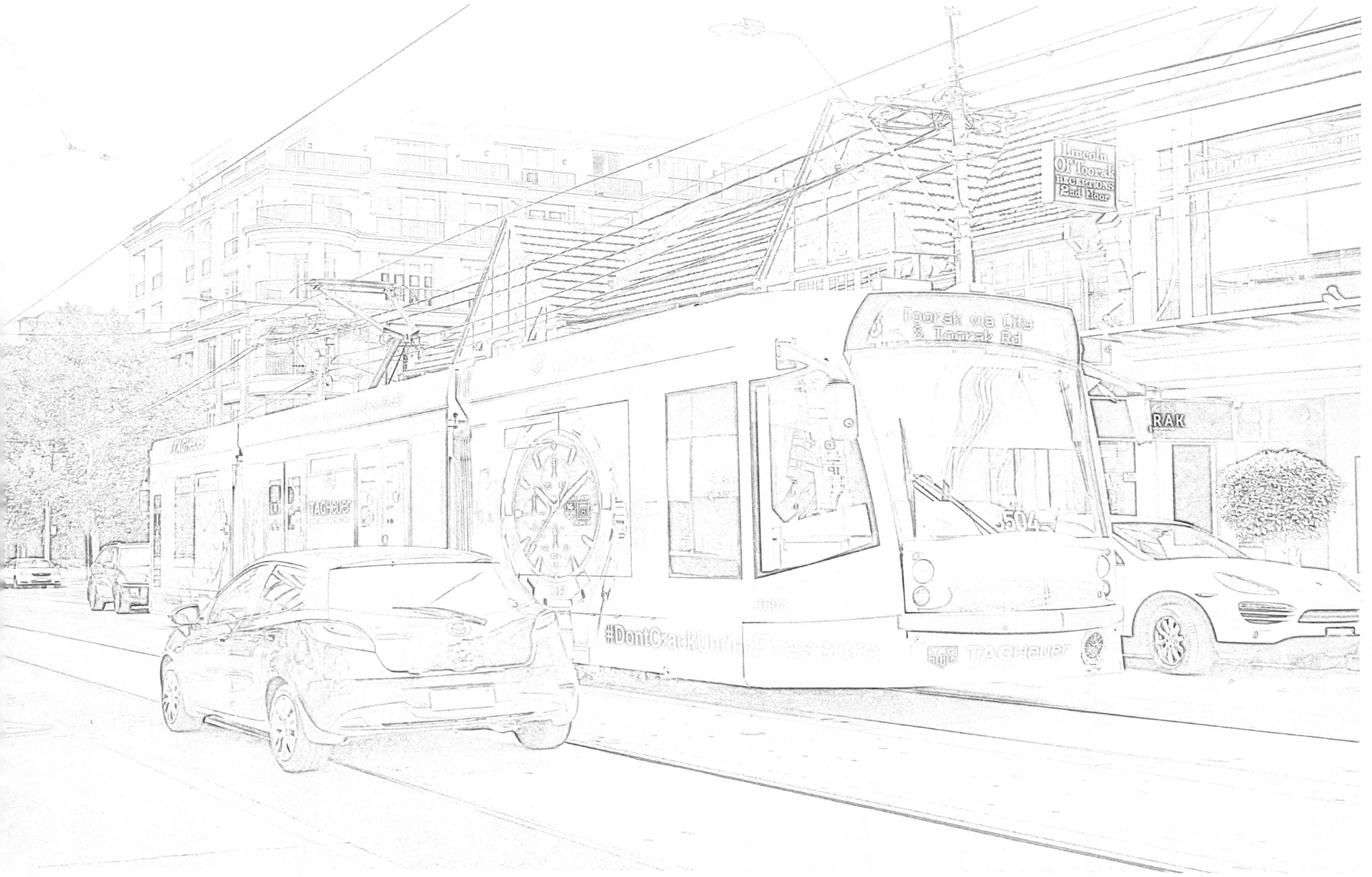
Lincoln
Of Toorak
RECEPTIONS
2nd Floor
Toorak via City
& Toorak Rd
3504
RAK
#DontCrackUnderPressure
TAGHeuer

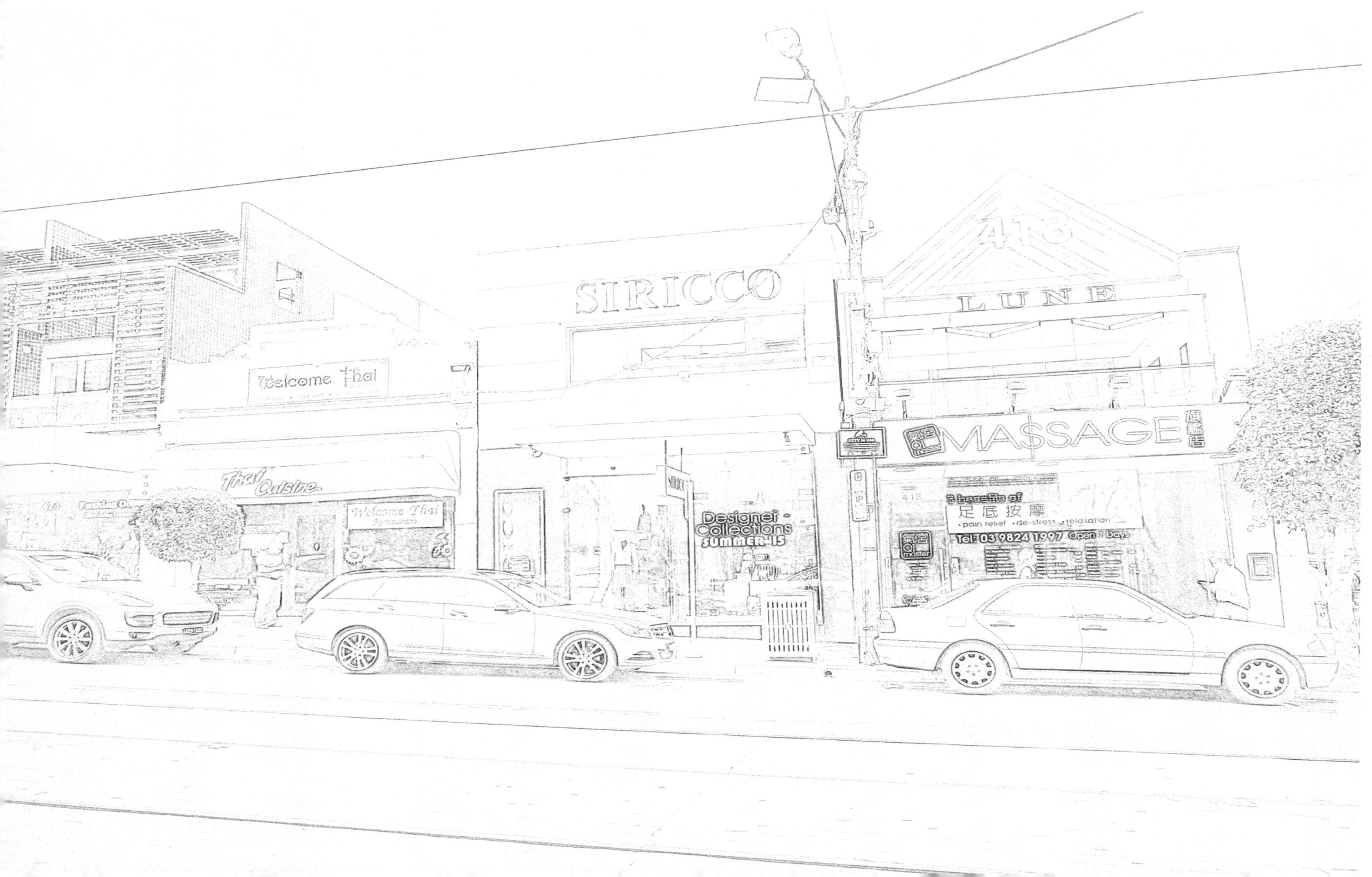
418
LUNE
SIRICCO
Welcome Thai
Thai Cuisine
Welcome Thai
Restaurant
MASSAGE
418
3 benefits of
足底按摩
• pain relief • de-stress • relaxation
Tel: 03 9824 1997 Open 7 Days
Designer Collections
SUMMER 15
424

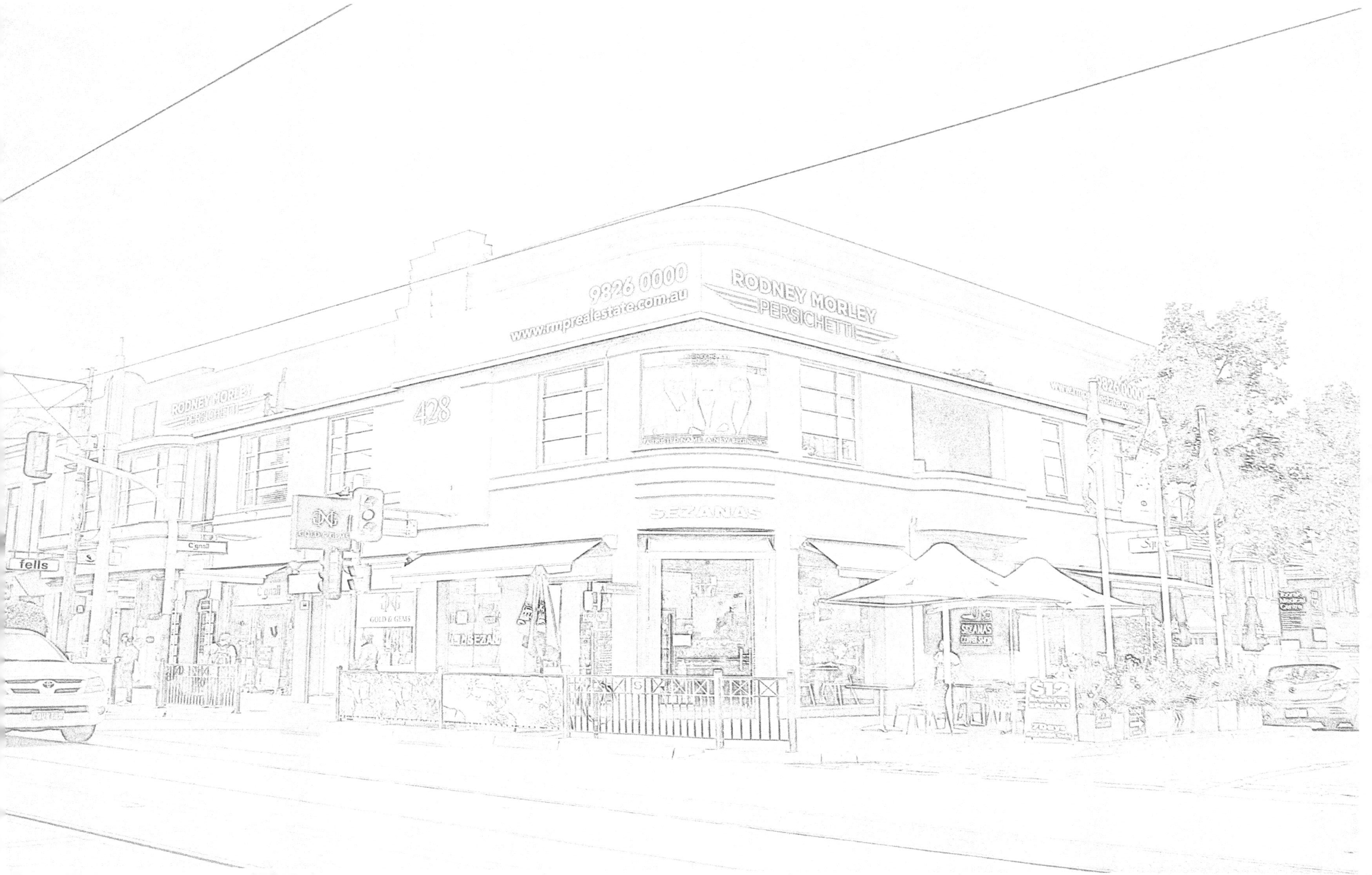

9826 0000
www.rmprealestate.com.au
RODNEY MORLEY
PERSICHETTI
428
A TRUSTED NAME A NEW BEGINNING
SEZANAS
GOLD & GEMS
fells
SEZANAS
$12

TRAFFIC
TRAFFIK
CLOSING DOWN
FINAL
TOORAK RD

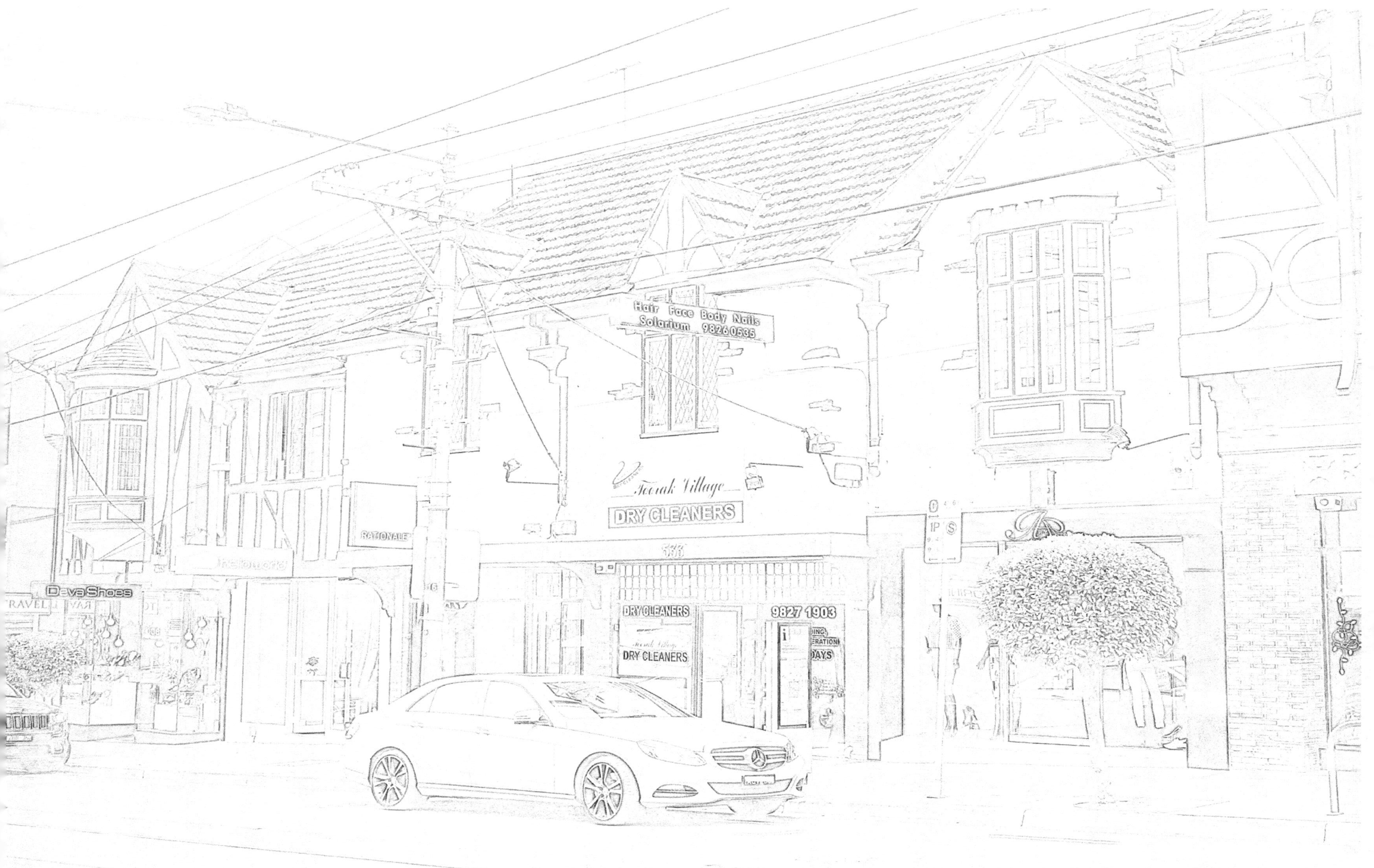
Hair Face Body Nails
Solarium 98260535
Toorak Village
DRY CLEANERS
DRY CLEANERS
9827 1903
Toorak Village
DRY CLEANERS
RATIONALE
DevaShoes
TRAVEL

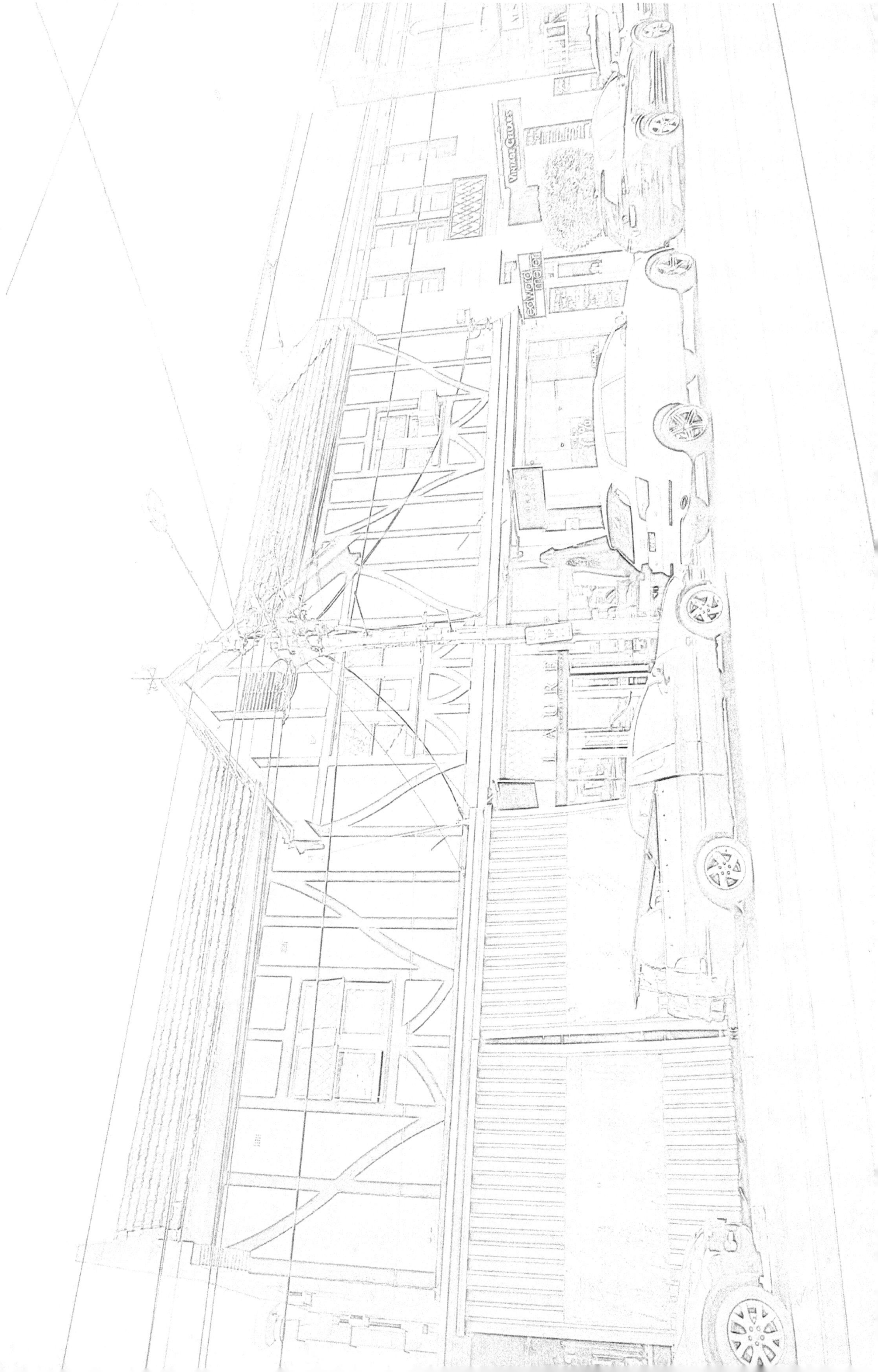

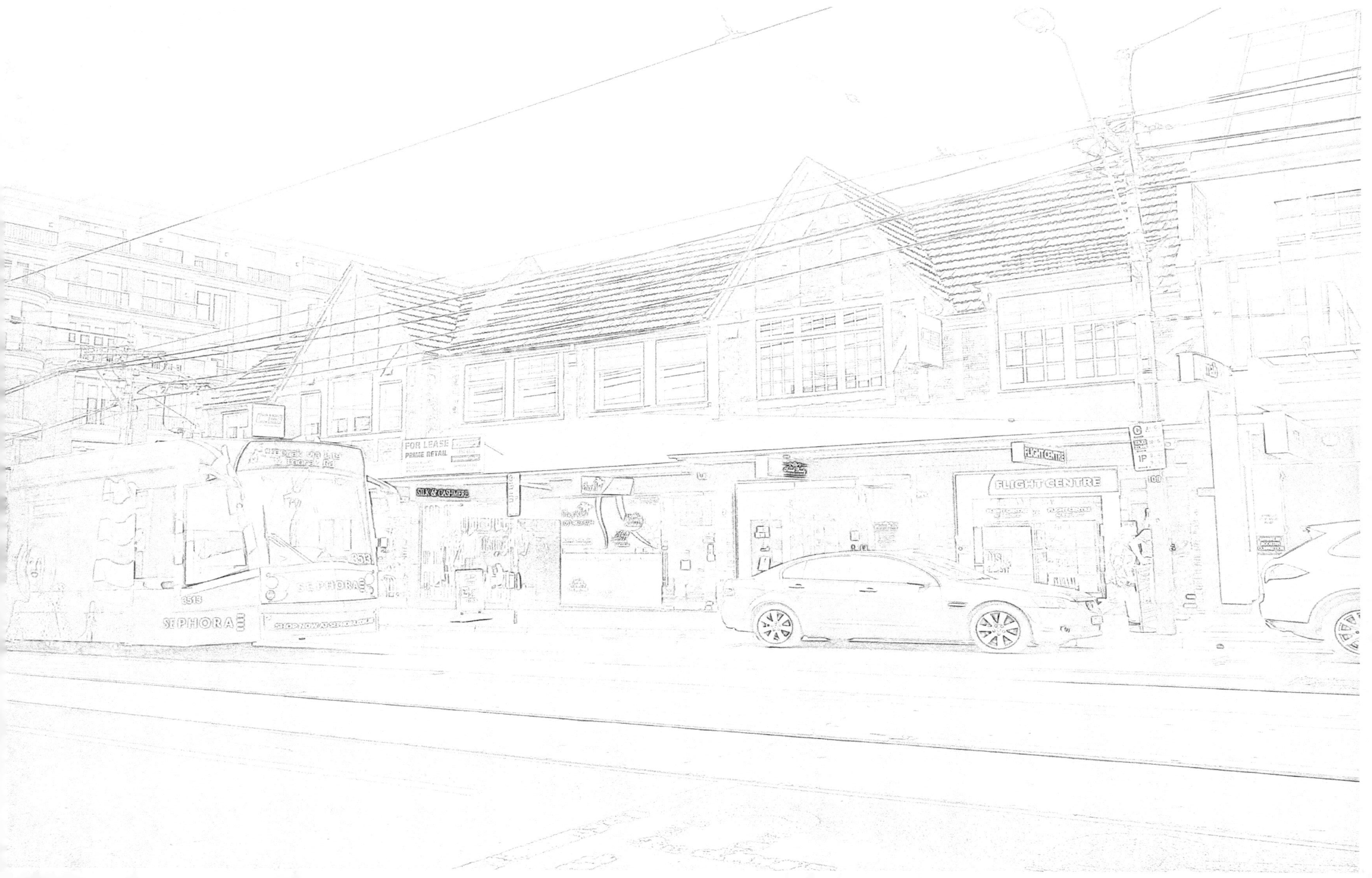

FOR LEASE
PRIME RETAIL
SILK & CASHMERE
FLIGHT CENTRE
FLIGHT CENTRE
SEPHORA
SEPHORA
3513

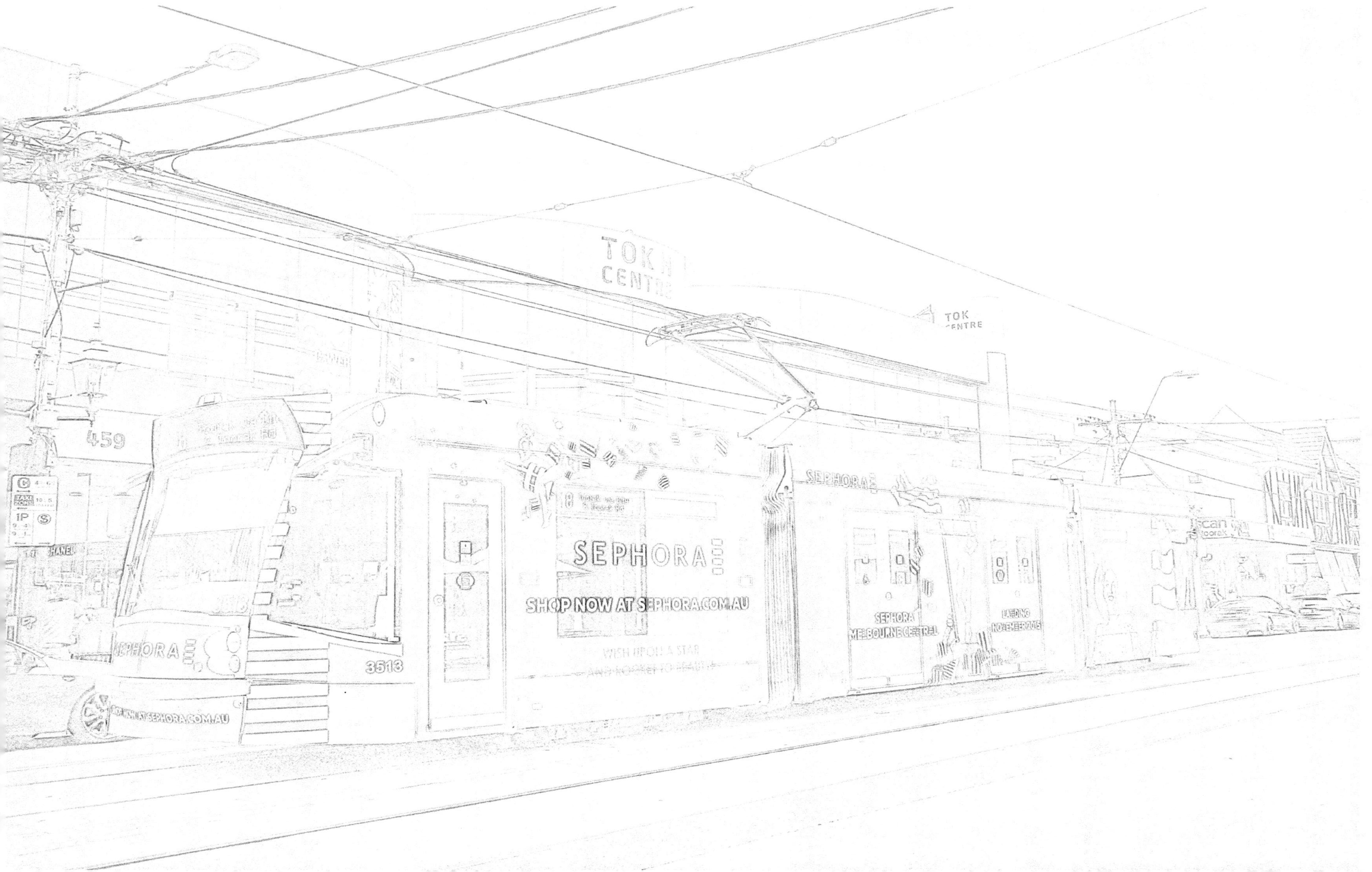
SEPHORA
SHOP NOW AT SEPHORA.COM.AU
3513
459
SEPHORA
SEPHORA
TOK
CENTRE

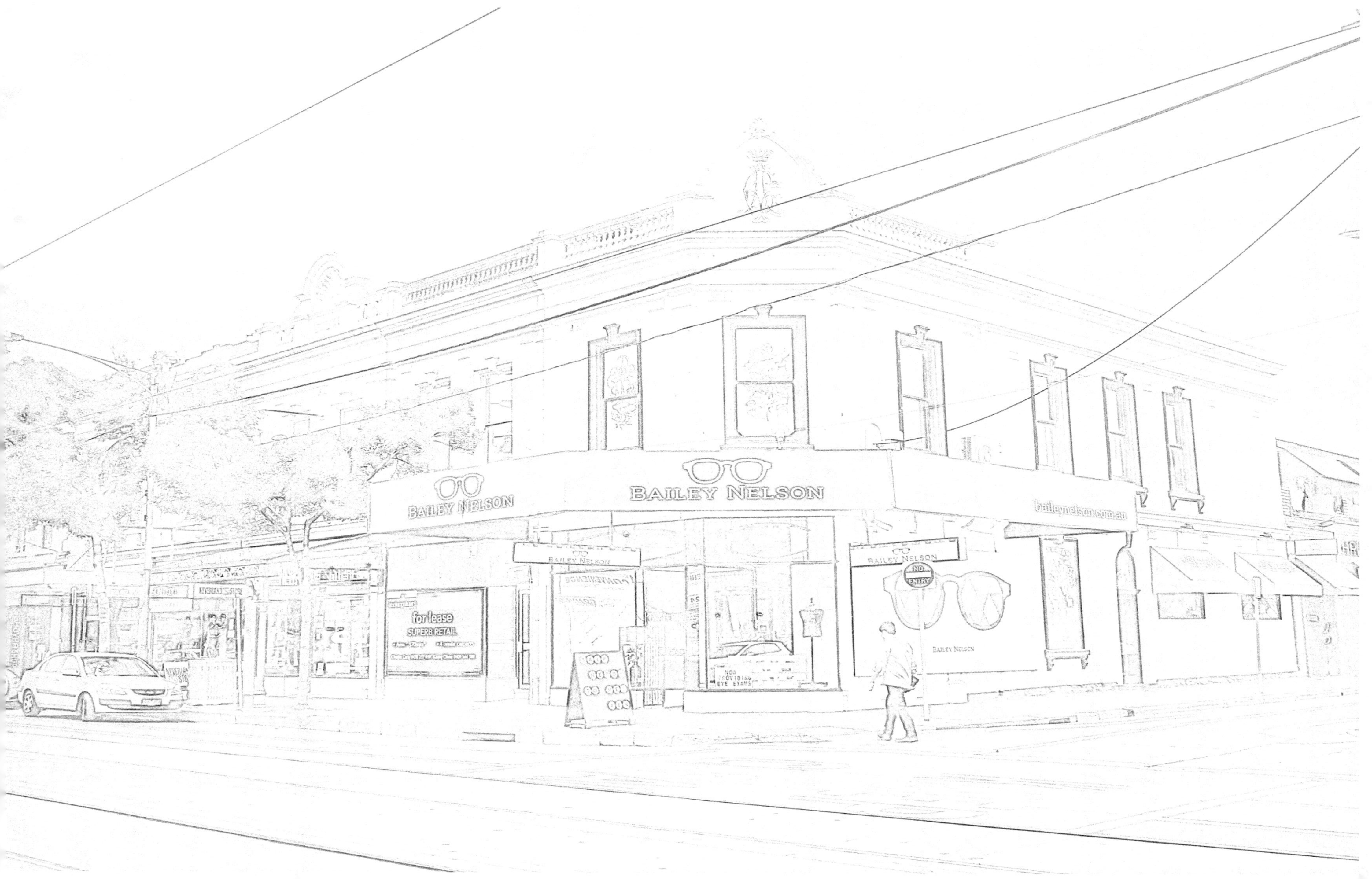

BAILEY NELSON
BAILEY NELSON
baileynelson.com.au
BAILEY NELSON
BAILEY NELSON
NO ENTRY
BAILEY NELSON
for lease
SUPERB RETAIL
NOW PROVIDING EYE EXAMS

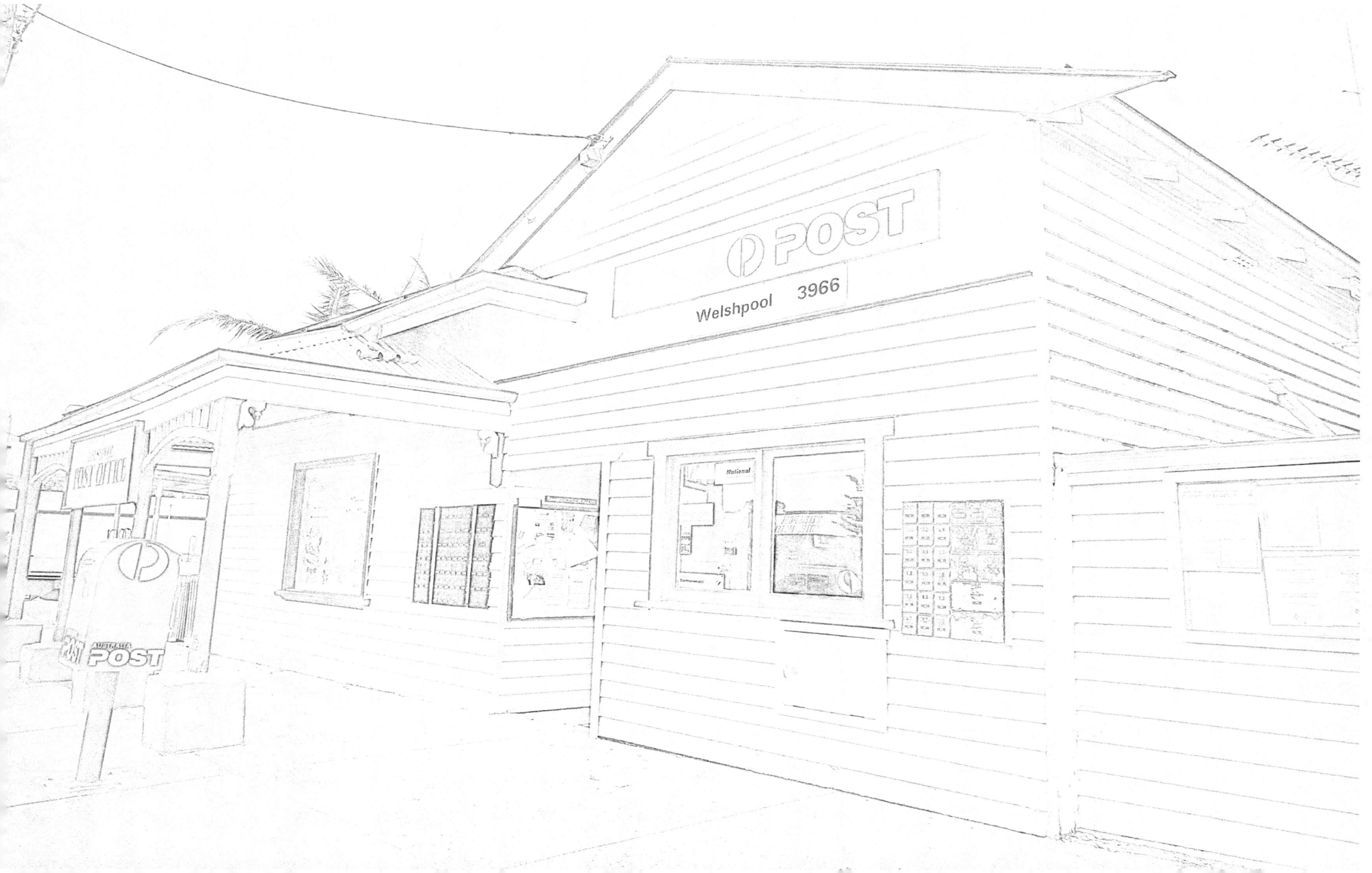
POST
Welshpool 3966
POST OFFICE
National
AUSTRALIA POST

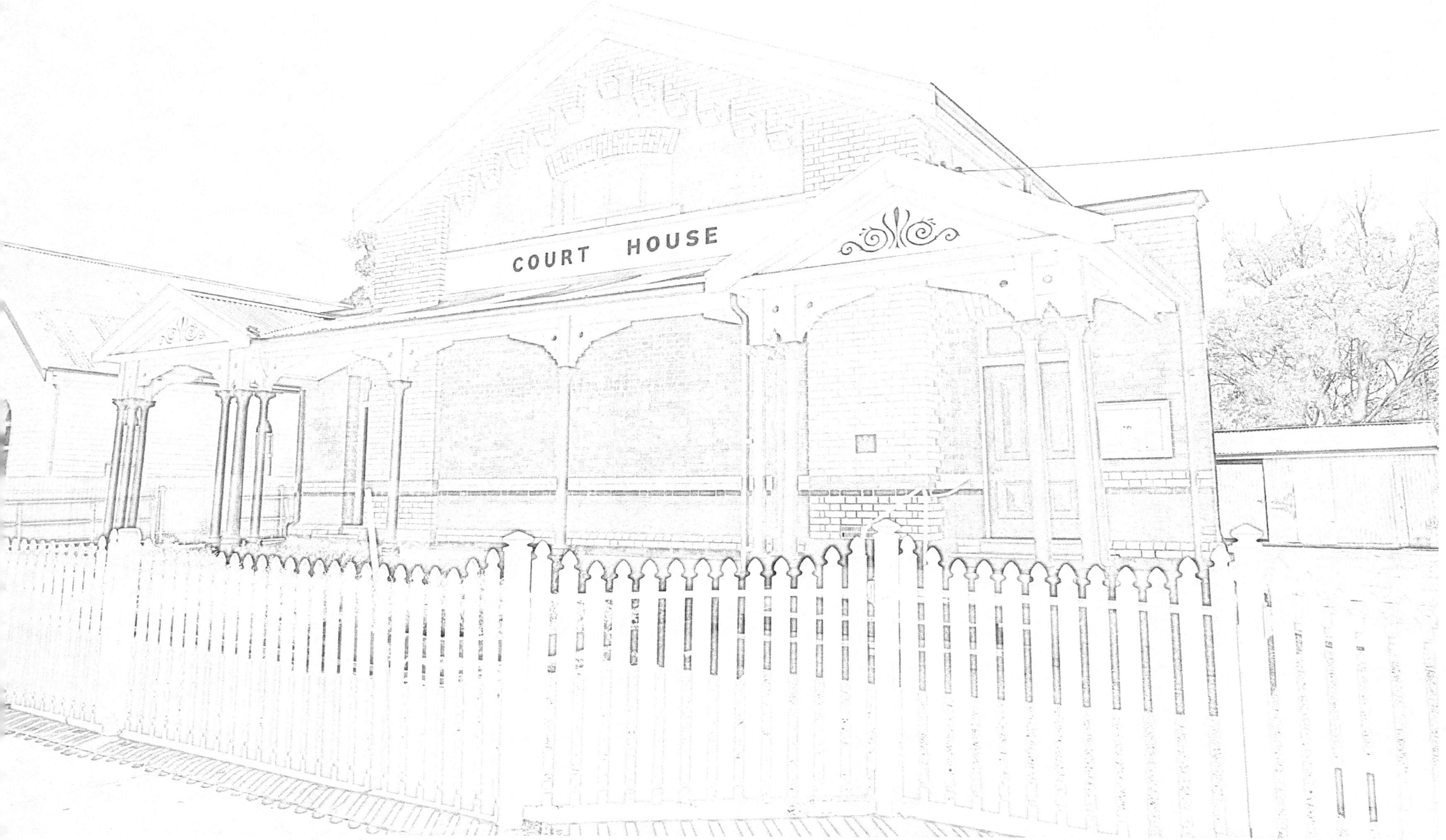
COURT HOUSE

www.ingramcontent.com/pod-product-compliance
Lightning Source LLC
Chambersburg PA
CBHW081057180526
45170CB00005B/1791
9780359865307